D0413174

HIDDEN
HAMPSHIRE

John Barton

with illustrations by
Anne-Louise Barton

COUNTRYSIDE BOOKS
NEWBURY, BERKSHIRE

COUNTRYSIDE BOOKS
3 Catherine Road
Newbury, Berkshire

ISBN 1 85306 049 6

Cover photograph of West Meon Railway Station
taken by Jeremy Barton

Line drawings by Anne-Louise Barton

Produced through MRM Associates, Reading
Typeset by Acorn Bookwork, Salisbury
Printed in England by J. W. Arrowsmith Ltd, Bristol

TO PAT
Who Saw Things I Missed

Introduction

This is the first guidebook to Hampshire that excludes most of the well-known sights such as country houses, parks, gardens, museums and ancient monuments. There is not much else to see if they are excluded, you may say, but you would be wrong for there are hundreds of hidden and curious things in out-of-the-way places that you may never have heard of. During the writing of this book I have discovered scores of intriguing sights that I never knew existed. In addition to things that can be seen I have included many little-known events and stories, some true and some not (and where not true I have said why not). Though in general well-known places are not mentioned, some little-known facts relating to a few of them have been included.

I have visited every village and small town in Hampshire and seen for myself everything described in this book. If you cannot find one of the objects or buildings I have written about then it has been destroyed since I saw it! Nearly everything in the book is visible from a public road or footpath, or is inside a church, and the few that are not are indicated 'no access' or 'private land'. I have not pin-pointed the exact whereabouts of every single thing in the book, for that would have made for tedious reading. Part of the pleasure to be derived from visiting these places will be in locating them for yourself, but I have in general pointed you in the right direction.

How did I choose which villages and towns to write about, out of about 300 in the county? It was a difficult task because nearly every village has something that is worth mentioning, but I finally reduced the number of entries to 160. Some places are included because they have an interesting history, some because they have hidden or curious buildings and objects, and some because an unusual event once took place there. Many places are included for all three reasons. It is perhaps appropriate that the village I have written most words about – Martin – is one of the most remote and little-known in Hampshire.

I have included the ten smallest towns in the county (Alton, Lymington, New Milton, Petersfield, Ringwood, Romsey, Tadley, Totton, Whitchurch and Yateley) because they are not much larger than some of the villages. I drew the line at a population of 21,000 in 1981, which excluded the eleven largest towns; there is enough 'hidden' in those large towns to warrant a book to themselves. To forestall queries as to what constitutes a 'town', I have defined it as a place that has a Town Council or a Borough Council as distinct from a Parish Council. I have also excluded Fleet, which does not have a Town Council but has a population of over 21,000.

Churches are often mentioned in this book, and to those not greatly interested in churches I apologise, but at the same time point out that a great deal of curious history can be found in churches and churchyards. I have not dwelt unduly on the architecture of churches, as this can be read in Pevsner and Lloyd's book or in *The Victoria History*. I have tried to draw attention to the strange and often overlooked aspects of many churches, and particularly to the curious memorials and monuments that can be seen inside and outside them. A parish church reflects the social and economic history of a village as no other building can hope to do, and a study of the stages in its building and extension, and of the people recorded in its memorials, can tell much about the past history of a village.

A few churches mentioned in the book will be found to be locked, an understandable precaution in these lawless times. Most of the locked churches display a notice giving the whereabouts of the key, but regrettably a minority of them have no such notice, a discourtesy to the many visitors who may have travelled miles to see the church. I have in the main omitted any mention in this book of that category of church; at the great majority of those I have written about the church is open or the key is available.

I should like to acknowledge the help I have received in writing this book from many individuals and organisations in the county. My special thanks I give to my wife Pat, who accompanied me on many journeys around Hampshire and read the whole of the manuscript, to Max Barton for help with Hawkley and Barton on Sea, and to Frank Green for a guided tour of Romsey. For help with particular queries or for permission to use published information I should like to thank Chris Currie, Robert Irwin, David Johnston, Edward Roberts,

Barry Shurlock, the Tadley and District Society, the Broughton Local History Society and the Botley and Curdridge Historical Society. My thanks also to Chris Burningham for the loan of church guidebooks. For general information and the answering of queries I am indebted to the staff of the Hampshire Local Studies Library, the Hampshire Record Office, the Royal Commission on Historical Monuments (Southampton) and the Hampshire Association of Parish Councils. Last but not least I thank my daughter Anne-Louise for the text illustrations, my son Jeremy for the cover photograph, and the publishers for their help and guidance. For any errors there may be I am entirely responsible.

John Barton

Abbotts Ann

➤ Ann or Anna was the old name for the stream (now the Pillhill brook) that meets the river Anton at Upper Clatford. In AD 901 the manor was granted to New Minster (later Hyde Abbey), Winchester, so the village name became Abbotts Ann.

In 1710 the manor passed to Thomas ('Diamond') Pitt, a former Governor of Madras and a shrewd businessman who had amassed a vast fortune, partly by selling a large diamond at a profit of £115,000 to the Regent of France. Pitt rebuilt St Mary's church in 1716; in only one other Hampshire church (Wolverton) is the early Georgian period so strongly evoked. Little has been altered since it was built – the pews (with hat-rests), the gallery on Tuscan columns and the pulpit are original.

St Mary's is the only church in England where the medieval custom of awarding virgins' crowns survives. The ceremony takes place at the funeral of an unmarried person of either sex who was born, baptised and confirmed in the parish, and who was a regular communicant of unblemished reputation. Each crown is made of hazel-wood and ornamented with paper rosettes. Attached to it are five parchment gauntlets, which represent a challenge to anybody who might dispute the good character of the deceased. After the funeral the crown is hung from the gallery for three weeks and then placed on a bracket near the ceiling, where it remains until it falls with age, some-times 200 years later.

In 1806 a young man named Robert Tasker arrived in Abbotts Ann. He started work with a local blacksmith, whose business he acquired three years later. He was so successful that in 1813 he opened a new foundry, which became the famous Waterloo Ironworks (see Upper Clatford). The smithy in Abbotts Ann has long since disappeared, but the house in which he lived is still there (No. 50). Next door he built a chapel, which was burnt down in 1899 together with the village school. Both were rebuilt; the chapel is now Chapel Cottage.

Alton

➤ Members of the Society of Friends, or Quakers as they became known, began meeting in Alton in about 1664; in 1672 they built the Quaker Meeting House in Church Street. The oldest Quaker meeting-house still in use in England, and probably in the world, is at Hertford and was built in 1670, so the one at Alton is probably the second oldest still in use in the world. Quakers at that time were much persecuted, until the Act of Toleration was passed in 1689. Set into the red bricks of the boundary wall are darker bricks that form the date 1672 – it can best be deciphered from the other side of the road.

A noted Quaker in later times was William Curtis (1746–99), the botanist and founder of the *Botanical Magazine*, who was born at No. 25 Lenten Street. The first issue of the magazine appeared in 1787 and was an instant success. The earlier annual volumes are now worth a lot of money and an almost complete set recently made £27,000 at auction.

When William Curtis was living in Alton a stage-coach named the Alton and Farnham Machine left the White Hart inn for London every Monday, Wednesday and Friday at 6.0 am, returning the next day. The fare was 10 shillings single for inside passengers and 5 shillings for outside passengers. By the early 19th century there were three coaches each way daily. An advertisement for the coach can be seen in The Curtis Museum.

A plaque on No. 1 Amery Street states that Edmund Spenser, the poet and author of *The Faerie Queene*, lived there in 1590. He had spent many years working in Ireland previous to that and in 1591 returned there after the publication of the first part of his famous epic.

A brass in St Lawrence's church commemorates the death of the Royalist 'Colonel Richard Boles' after a fierce battle inside the church in '1641'. His name was really John Bolle and the date was 1643. Bullet-holes and pike-marks made by the attacking Roundheads can be seen in the south door. This was probably the most momentous event in Alton's history; the loss of the town to the Parliamentarians was a major blow to the Royalists.

An event of a quite different kind, which made national news at the time and gave a phrase to our language, occurred in 1867. 'Killed a young girl. It was fine and hot.' That matter-of-fact entry in a diary was the main evidence in the conviction of a solicitor's clerk named Frederick Baker for the murder of an eight-year-old girl named Fanny Adams. He had taken her one afternoon to a field not far from her home in Tanhouse Lane and cut her into many pieces. It was the first murder ever recorded in Alton and one of the most gruesome ever committed in England. Baker admitted his guilt but gave no reason for the crime. His execution in Winchester was attended by 5,000 people from all over the county. One wonders how many people would attend a public hanging today.

Tinned meat was then being issued to the Royal Navy as an experiment. In disgust at its poor quality and with the macabre humour of the lower deck it was nicknamed 'sweet Fanny Adams'. With a change of meaning the phrase has now passed into the language as slang for 'nothing'.

Amport

➤ The school and almshouses opposite the village green were paid for by Sophia, the widow of Thomas Sheppard, rector of Basingstoke for 46 years, who died a wealthy man. He was 73 and she only 31 years old when they were married.

The school was opened in 1815 (inscription on the pediment) and endowed in 1816 (inscription on the end wall). By 1880 there were nearly 100 pupils – in one room with no whispering allowed. On May Day each child received a penny and a currant bun. The villagers insisted on celebrating May Day on 12th May instead of 1st May because, as in some other rural areas, they would not accept the Gregorian calendar, thinking it would deprive them of eleven days!

The Sheppard Almshouses were built in 1815 for six poor widows (inscription on the pediment), who each received £2 every month. These almshouses saved many a poor woman from having to enter the infamous Andover workhouse. One of the houses is still marked 'Chapel'.

The 18th-century cottages facing the green (eg Willow Cottage 1711) are not only attractive and varied – no two are alike – but also interesting in that they reflect the changing fortunes of ownership in that century. When they were first built some were owned by labourers, but it became increasingly difficult for labourers to save money because wages were kept down by the rise in population, so many of the cottages were bought by farmers who let them to their workers. Rosemary Cottage was originally divided into three houses – the middle one was sold for £5 in 1715.

The discontent among farm labourers culminated in 1830 in riots, when rampaging mobs of agricultural workers burned hayricks and broke farm machinery all over the south of England. Their demands for an increase in wages (from eight shillings to twelve shillings a week) were generally granted, though later nine of the ringleaders were hung and about 450 transported. But wages in Amport a year later were down to ten shillings a week and in 1846 were down to eight shillings a week again.

St Mary's church is that rarity in Hampshire – a church in the Decorated style, even though it is largely Victorian Decorated; it was restored in 1866–7. It has one curious relic, a medieval St John the Baptist's Head, made of alabaster at Nottingham. The largest of the St John's Heads in England, it was found in a local cottage and may have been an altar-piece in a wayside chapel.

Ashley

The little village of Ashley is only a few miles from Winchester but is quite remote and unspoilt. St Mary's church stands inside the bailey of a Norman castle, the only church in that position in Hampshire (Portchester church is inside a Roman fort). The simple two-celled church, now redundant, has a Norman chancel arch and south doorway. The chancel is as long as the nave but obviously has been lengthened at some time. The castle is probably the one that was fortified by licence in 1200 by William Briwere; it is typically Norman with its outer bailey and strong ramparts. King John stayed at Ashley with his friend William Briwere when he came here on hunting expeditions.

There is a memorial to Thomas Hobbs, physician to three kings (Charles II, James II and William III), and a classical memorial to Abraham Weekes, a man of impeccable character if we are to believe his epitaph. A unique Elizabethan alms-box has apparently been made from a wooden post.

The gravestone to Maria Caplin (died 1889) reads:

> Stranger pause ere you pass by.
> Is you are now so once was I.
> Is I am now so you must be.
> Prepare at once to follow me.

In the village street there is an old timber-framed and thatched well-head dating from 1616, in reasonable condition for its age.

Ashmansworth

➤ Ashmansworth is the highest-situated village in Hampshire; at The Plough public house you are 770 ft above sea-level (and about 3° Fahrenheit cooler!). The village extends for more than a mile along the top of a ridge, and is only two miles from the highest point in Hampshire (see East Woodhay). As one would expect in this remote northern part of the county the village is very quiet; its old thatched cottages make it attractive but not ostentatiously so.

St James's church has several medieval wall-paintings, but they have faded so much that they are rather difficult to decipher. Gerald Finzi, the composer, is buried here; his tombstone was engraved by the artist Reynolds Stone. His memorial window in the porch, engraved by Laurence Whistler, depicts a tree with its roots ending in the initials of 50 famous English composers.

The Ox Drove (see East Woodhay) forms part of the parish boundary on the north-east, and the ancient Priests' Way, which is said to have connected the churches between Combe and Litchfield, crosses the village street.

Barton on Sea

➤ In 1870 there were only nine cottages at Barton, as it was known then, plus the row of six coastguard cottages still to be seen in Barton Lane. It developed rapidly between the wars as a place for retirement.

The obelisk at the seaward end of Barton Court Avenue commemorates the establishment in 1914 of a convalescent depot for Indian troops who fought in the First World War. They occupied the Grand Marine Hotel, now Barton Chase, on the sea-front. The Dome Hotel, with its oriental gold dome appropriately overlooking the Indian memorial, was formerly The Barton Tea House, one of the first restaurants here.

A stone set into No. 70 Sea Road records that the house was once used by Marconi as a wireless telephone station in his experiments with aircraft communication.

Barton Court, all that remains of a much larger building, once had spacious grounds between it and the sea; now it is only a few feet from the cliff-top. If the main part of the house had not been removed in 1922 because of the danger of cliff erosion, it would have fallen down the cliff by now.

The Barton Beds, famous for fossils, got their name from Barton on Sea; the sands and clays forming the beds, which are nearly 200 ft thick here, are exposed in the cliff-face. A walk along the beach will take you to many spots where the bottom of the cliff has been eroded, causing oversteepening of the angle of the cliff-face and consequent landslips. Erosion in recent years has been particularly marked just east of Chewton Bunny as a result of incomplete coastal protection.

Beaulieu

➤ Beaulieu (=beautiful place), though famous because of the Motor Museum and abbey, is a modest place. It caters for its visitors discreetly, as befits such a charming and well-kept village. It does have gift shops, such as Beaulieu Chocolate Parlour and Secrets of the Forest, but they are not of the ostentatious kind that disfigure some places in Hampshire.

The parish church was once the refectory of the abbey and is orientated north-south, which probably makes it unique among English parish churches. The pulpit from which readings were given to the monks at meal times is a rare survival. The church should be visited before twelve noon if that is your only reason for visiting Beaulieu; after then you will have to pay for entrance to the Motor Museum in order to visit the church, which certainly makes it unique.

A public footpath from The Montagu Arms Hotel takes you to Bailey's Hard, where some buildings and a chimney of the old brick and tile works survive; the footpath goes on to Bucklers Hard.

Beyond Bucklers Hard is St Leonards Grange, where you can see the remains of one of the largest tithe barns in England, originally measuring about 216 ft by 60 ft. An idea of its size can be had from the present barn, which covers about one-quarter of the area of the old tithe barn. Wool produced on the Beaulieu estate was stored in the tithe barn before being exported.

In 1826 William Cobbett was misdirected to St Leonards after asking the way to Beaulieu Abbey. He soon realised that he had been misinformed but nevertheless wrote afterwards that it was 'a thousand times finer place than that where the Abbey . . . really stood. . . . the place is one of the finest that ever was seen in this world.' High praise indeed, but a typical piece of Cobbett exaggeration.

Further west is Sowley Pond, a large fishpond made by the monks of Beaulieu (see Titchfield). It was later used to provide water-power for an ironworks on the opposite side of the road, where the forge was working until about 1822.

Beaulieu is 'twinned' with Hautvillers, a village south of Reims more famous to the French than to us. Its church was part of the Benedictine abbey in which Dom Perignon is said to have developed the art of making 'sparkling' champagne, which gave rise to a new wine industry.

Bentley

➤ The village sign, in the form of a large wooden 'book', was designed it is said by Lord Baden-Powell for the *Daily Mail* Village Signs Competition in 1923. He lived at Pax Hill from 1918 to 1938, when he retired to Kenya. The Bentley sign did not win first prize but it should certainly have gained an award for the weird and wonderful 'historical' information displayed on it. Surmounting the book is the figure of 'Willm ye Archer of ye Green by ye Forest' (see below). The information is divided into two sections, 'Points of Interest' and 'History of Bentley'.

Points of interest. 1. *Bentley means the 'Green by the Forest'*. The name is derived from Old English *beonet-leah*, meaning 'clearing overgrown with bent' (bent is a type of grass). There was a forest here (part of Alice Holt), but it is not recorded in the place-name. 2. *The Manor was assigned in Doomsday Book* (sic) *to William the Archer*. The manor of Bentley assigned in Domesday Book to William the Archer was not this Bentley but the one at Mottisfont. This manor of Bentley was held by the Bishop of Winchester in 1086 so William the Archer has no connection with this Bentley. 3. *The Church Norman Unique*. Parts of the church are indeed Norman but in no way unique. 4. *Avenue of Yews probably originated when Bentley supplied an Archer to the King each year*. This is unlikely. 5. *East Window Glass dated 1452*. The east window glass is mainly Victorian but also has fragments dating from the 15th century, which cannot be dated as precisely as 1452. 6. *The Tin Highway used by Phoenicians from Cornwall to Thanet ran just north of Bentley*. This may refer to the Harrow Way, one of the oldest roads in Britain, which ran from the West Country to the Kent coast near Dover. There is no firm evidence that the Phoenicians ever came to Cornwall to collect tin and they certainly did not take it to Thanet, or collect it from Thanet, or have any reason for visiting Thanet. 7. *The Pilgrims Way Winchester to Canterbury ran via Coldrey House & Holy well near the Church*. The Pilgrims' Way followed roughly the course of the modern main road, near Coldrey but not near the church, though undoubtedly pilgrims made a detour to it. 8. *Roman pavements found at Coldrey & Barley Pound*. A Roman mosaic pavement was found at Barley Pound Farm in 1817, but there was no pavement in the remains of the Roman buildings discovered at Coldrey. 9. *Ancient Fort Norman & possibly British at Barley Pound.* This refers to the earthworks of a Norman castle. 10. *Pass at Alton 1½ miles west of Coldrey was infested by Robbers.* Most highways were. 11. *Marelands, Gilbert White, Naturalist stayed here.* In 1793, not long before he died, Gilbert White visited his brother at Marelands. 12. *Alice Holt Oak Forest maintained for Government Shipbuilding.* True. 13. *Q. Victoria Stone on site of Malefactors Cage & Stocks.* The obelisk stands near the cottages named The Cage.

History of Bentley. *41 AD Roman Occupation.* It is interesting to learn that the Romans were in Bentley two years before they invaded Britain! *500 Saxon. 1001 Danes fought English near here.* True. The *Anglo-Saxon Chronicle* records that at Alton 'then came there against them the men of Hampshire and fought against them' (in AD 1001). *1086 Normans held Bentley.* True. *1400 Church Restored. Registers started 1563.* The church was restored about 1400; the first register dates from 1538. *1643 Basing House attacked by troops after Inspection on Bentley Green by Sir Waller.* (William Waller.) *1651–9 Marriages celebrated here during Commonwealth. Most chuches* (sic) *having ceased using Prayer Book.* True. The use of the Book of Common Prayer was prohibited for baptisms, funerals and marriages. A marriage had to take place in front of a Justice of the Peace, but most couples had a religious ceremony afterwards as well. *1914–19 The Great War Bentley furnished 131 men out of a population of 671, of whom 23 did not return. 1923 The Memorial Hall, built on a site presented by Tho's Eggar was open* (sic) *by the Chief Scout Gen. Sir Robert Baden Powell Bart, who lived at Pax Hill. 1939–45 The Second World War 16 Men did not Return. The Memorial in the Church which Records their Names unveiled by F.M. Viscount Montgomery in 1949.*

Binsted

➤ Oast-houses are conspicuous in Binsted, which was once the centre of a prosperous hop-growing area. They make an attractive picture whether in their original state or when converted to other uses. There are several old brick and timber-framed houses in Binsted, notably the group facing Holy Cross church. The thatched White Hart was formerly an inn, and The Cedars public house opposite apparently caters only for locals ('No Travellers').

In the churchyard is the grave of Field Marshal Viscount Montgomery of Alamein (1887–1976). He spent his last years at Isington Mill, a beautiful spot on the river Wey; the large wooden building in the garden once contained his wartime caravans. Other memorials in the church include an effigy of Richard de Westcote, a Crusader knight (c.1332), and a brass to Henry, son of Richard Heighes (1595). The churchwardens' accounts for 1715 on display include charges for 'whiping ye doggs' – 6 shillings, 'binding ye Church Bible' – 19 shillings, and 'bell-roops' – £1.10s.0d.

Bishop's Waltham

If you walk round Bishop's Waltham with John Bosworth's books of old photographs, which show the streets as they were in the 19th and early 20th century, you will find that many of the buildings are immediately recognisable, but at the same time you will find that many have disappeared. The character of the streets has changed more rapidly in recent years with the erection of new buildings and the modernisation of old ones. That may not be a bad thing, for 30 years ago Bishop's Waltham was by all accounts run-down, indeed many buildings were almost falling down.

Bishop's Waltham has never achieved urban status but it has been an important market centre since medieval times, with an early rectangular street layout. It is quite possible that the whole of the area now bounded by Brook Street, Bank Street and Houchin Street was once a large market square, and that only since the 18th century has it been built upon with houses and shops. The many narrow east-west alleys in this area are intriguing.

Three streets deserve special mention. St Peter's Street is an attractive cul-de-sac ending at the churchyard. The east side of

Basingwell Street consists of an almost unbroken sequence of 17th- and 18th-century colour-washed cottages and houses, one of the best street vistas in Hampshire; the line is broken by the ugly St Paul's Primitive Methodist church of 1910 – two old cottages were demolished to make way for it!

Bank Street (formerly French Street) was renamed when the Bishop's Waltham & Hampshire Bank (later called Gunner's Bank) commenced business there in 1809 – the old bank building is on the north side, opposite Malvern Close. When Gunner's was taken over by Barclays Bank in 1953 it was the last private country bank in England. Also in Bank Street are the Institute, built in 1898 to provide a library and reading-room, The Mafeking Hero public house (renamed in 1901 – previously The White Hart), and The Old Granary with its modern craft workshops.

The Crown in St George's Square is an old coaching inn; it lost its courtyards when the bypass was built. It once had a door that was called the 'mortuary door' because of the large number of road victims that were carried through it. When main road traffic came through St George's Square the corner by the inn was a particularly dangerous spot.

Bishop's Waltham once had a railway station. It stood where the roundabout is now and was surprisingly large for a branch line that went no further. The line was a single track from Botley and it was hoped at one time to make it a through line to Droxford on the Meon Valley line. It was opened in 1863 and was closed to passengers in 1933 and to goods in 1962. One of the crossing-gates and a short length of track have been preserved near the roundabout.

St Peter's church has been restored so often over the years that it has lost much of its character. It is interesting that the tower (1584–9), the north aisle (1637) and the south aisle (1652) were rebuilt in the Gothic tradition, a late survival of that style, when elsewhere the classical style was coming into fashion. Old furnishings include a pulpit of 1626, a west gallery of 1733 with its original box-pews, and a font that could be Saxon in date. There is a memorial to Admiral of the Fleet Viscount Cunningham, whose home was at Palace House from 1936 to 1963.

In the 19th century a pottery works was built at Claylands; it became the most important in Hampshire. Skilled pottery workers were brought from Staffordshire, and a row of houses built for some of them can be seen in Albert Road, Newtown. Some of the terracotta products from the factory are in the museum in Brook Street (open on Sunday afternoons in summer).

An interesting exhibit in the museum is the toll-board from Park Lane Gate on the Bishop's Waltham and Fisher's Pond turnpike road of 1833. The first charge reads: 'For every Horse or other Beast, drawing any Coach, Chariot, Landau, Berlin, Chaise, Chair, Curricle, Calash, Hearse or other such Carriage not being a Stage Coach, Machine, Caravan or Diligence the sum of 3d.' It seems to have covered all possible conveyances of the time, to make sure that the well-to-do paid up, but one would think that hearses would have been exempt as a token of reverence to the dead.

The level crossing gates at Bishop's Waltham

Boarhunt

➤ According to Ekwall (*The Oxford Dictionary of English Place-Names*) the name has nothing to do with boars or hunting but was first recorded as Old English *Byrhfunt*, which means 'spring by the fort or town'. The church and farm are indeed situated on the chalk downs where a spring might issue, but there is no record of a fortified place. There is no village now, but one was mentioned in Domesday Book.

The small Anglo-Saxon church here on the north slope of Ports Down seems quite remote yet it is in fact only two miles from Fareham. It has been precisely dated to the year 1064 and is little changed since that time. Inside the building one can visualise the villagers attending service in their new church, little knowing that their routine existence was soon to be rudely upset by the Normans. The plain unmoulded chancel arch is the dominant feature, its narrowness typical of Saxon architecture.

The furnishings are Victorian, dating from the restoration of 1853, yet they include a three-decker pulpit, a squire's pew and a west gallery, the very things that were then being systematically destroyed in many churches in the name of ecclesiology and the Gothic Revival. It could only have been because this church was so isolated that it not only escaped relatively unscathed from Victorian restoration but also actually installed those items that were anathema nearly everywhere else.

The monument of 1577 to the Henslow family is an example of a new type of monument that appeared in the later 16th century, a type without figures but with classical ornament. Corinthian columns support a large entablature and three pediments with statues of Faith, Hope and Charity. How appropriate to find a monument heralding the end of the Gothic era in a church that in the 19th century would have nothing to do with the Gothic Revival.

Nelson's Monument was erected on Ports Down in 1807 by those who served under him at Trafalgar. The inscription records that the British fleet consisted of 27 ships of the line, and that of France and Spain 33, 19 of which were taken or destroyed.

Boldre

◤ When William Gilpin became vicar of Boldre in 1777 he found the inhabitants living in primitive conditions and leading lives of complete lawlessness. He decided to reform them, by setting an example of honest living and by establishing a village school and a poorhouse.

But that was not the reason he became famous. He was the first writer to outline and develop the idea of picturesqueness and beauty in nature and landscape, and wrote several books on the subject, notably *Remarks on Forest Scenery, and other Woodland Views* (1791). He illustrated the books himself with drawings that gave his impressions of the countryside. He had the gift of being able to describe a picturesque landscape, and he set down in his books the required standards of scenery that would satisfy aesthetic tastes.

He founded the village school in 1791, and in 1802 he endowed it with the proceeds of an auction sale of many of his drawings and manuscripts, which realised £1,558 (equivalent to about £50,000 today). The old school is now Gilpin's Cottage, and the memorial tablet from it, now inside the school at Pilley, reads: 'For the instruction of the children of Day Labourers of Boldre, this school was endowed by William Gilpin, many years Vicar of the Parish. He died April 5th, 1804, aged 80 years.'

Gilpin wrote an account of the school and its methods of instruction; the differential treatment of the boys and the girls makes odd reading today.

'The chief employment of the girls is knitting, sewing, mending their clothes, cleaning the house, and other little pieces of housewifery which may fit them for being useful in the world. The boys are taught writing, and arithmetic as far as the four first rules. To the girls, writing and arithmetic may occasionally be of use, but are not so generally useful as the domestic employments, on which their time is more engaged.'

It should be noted that both boys and girls were expected to be able to read before being admitted to the school.

Gilpin's vicarage was the house at Vicar's Hill now named

Gilpins. He is buried in the churchyard with his wife; the inscription on his tomb (composed by him) reads:

'In a quiet mansion beneath this stone, secured from the affliction and the still more dangerous enjoyments of life, lie the remains of William Gilpin, sometime Vicar of this Parish, together with the remains of Margaret his wife. . . . . Here it will be a joy to see several of their good neighbours who now lie scattered in these sacred precincts around them.'

It has been suggested that his use of the word 'several' meant that there were some neighbours he did not look forward to meeting!

Gilpin's curate at one time was Richard Warner, also a writer of some distinction. He published in 1795 the first great history of the county, entitled *Collections for the History of Hampshire*. Robert Southey was married to his second wife Caroline Bowles in St John's church in 1839; he was Poet Laureate at the time.

The memorials in the church to HMS *Hood*, the warship that sank in 1941 with only three survivors, include a painting of the ship, two lanterns and two carved oak benches. Vice-Admiral Holland, whose flagship it was, had been a regular worshipper at the church.

The Old School House in Boldre Lane was formerly an infants school. On it is a plaque that reads:

'In thankful memory of deliverance from Brigands of the Province of Salerno in Italy by payment of a ransom of L.5100 after 102 days' captivity, in the year 1865 W.J.C. Moens of Tweed Esqre. Erected this Church of England School AD 1869'.

The school was built with the profits from the book *English Travellers and Italian Brigands* (1866), in which Moens described his capture. Adjoining the old school is The Old Post Office, which retains the old letter-box in its front wall.

The signboard of The Hobler public house on the Brocken-hurst–Lymington road depicts a man with a horse. A 'hobby' was a small or medium-sized horse, and a 'hobbler' (correct spelling) was a family servant who had to keep a hobby for military service, or a soldier who rode a hobby. The word in that sense is now obsolete (except on inn-signs!).

Botley

In 1805 William Cobbett moved to Botley with his family, to a house with gardens sloping down to the river. Botley House, as Cobbett called it, stood at the end of the modern Hamblewood; a picture of it is in Southampton Museum library. The house was destroyed soon after Cobbett left Botley but Cobbett's House and Cobbett's Cottage, which are on the east side of Church Lane, were once part of his estate. He described Botley as 'the most delightful village in the world'.

Later for financial reasons he sold this house and rented Sherecroft House, which stands on the main road just east of Botley Mill. A stone opposite the mill records that Cobbett 'lived in Botley near this spot circa 1805–1817'. This memorial was the idea of the Hampshire members of the Institute of Journalists, in memory of one of England's greatest journalists.

Delightful as Cobbett found it, Botley must have been a noisy place at times, for it once had 14 inns to cater for the passing coach trade. Several of them were in High Street; only two survive, The Bugle Inn and The Dolphin.

There were two mills in Botley at the time of Domesday Book, and the present mill stands on the site of one of them. It is said to be the only mill in Hampshire mentioned in Domesday Book that is still producing flour.

Bramdean

Bramdean means 'the valley where broom grows'. The name was first recorded in AD 932, but long before then there was a Roman villa here, a mile east of the present village; it was excavated in 1823. The medieval village may have been near the church.

There are three outstanding houses in the village, The Old Rectory, with a mansard roof on one wing, Bramdean House, early 18th century, and Bramdean Manor near the church, of about 1740. The Fox Inn announces proudly that it gave shelter and hospitality to the Prince of Wales in 1780 (he was then 18

The church in the Wood, Bramdean Common

years old). Perhaps as well that it is not known for sure what he had been doing in this part of the world!

The church has some early features but was obviously over-restored in Victorian times. The chancel arch is late Norman – it is slightly pointed, heralding the advent of the Gothic arch. The first rector we know of (in 1289) was Giles the Englishman, a descriptive name of mysterious significance; in those days many priests were foreigners.

A circle of stones by the side of the main road at The Dean is often mistaken for a prehistoric stone circle. The stones were in fact placed there by a Colonel Greenwood as a memorial to one of his favourite horses.

On Bramdean Common, hidden in the woods, stands a picturesque little corrugated-iron church, known as the Church in the Wood. It was erected in 1883 for the gypsies who then camped in some numbers on the common, and took only five weeks to build. There are no gypsies there now but the church still has services in the summer. Magdalen College, Oxford, the owners of the land, receive an annual rent of five pence.

Bramley

➤ There are many interesting things in St James's church; it has one of the best-furnished interiors in Hampshire. The gallery dates from 1735, the bench-ends are quite ancient and the restored 15th-century screen has five-light divisions unique in Hampshire. The wall-paintings include one of St Christopher (opposite the blocked-up south doorway) and one of the murder of Thomas Becket. There is much old stained glass, including seven small English mid-14th-century figures and some of the Liège School of 1480–1520.

The Manor House in Vyne Road has a half-timbered front and is of the hall-house type with a recessed front and two projecting wings, which have carved barge-boards on the gables. This fine example of a 16th-century house can be studied at leisure because it fronts on to the road.

Bramshott

➤ Bramshott parish includes a rare diversity of intriguing places – Bramshott village, Liphook, Hammer Bottom, Waggoners Wells, Ludshott Common, Passfield Common, Conford, and part of Woolmer Forest, more than enough to visit in one day.

On its east side three counties meet (Hampshire, Surrey and West Sussex), one of the four points on the Hampshire border where this occurs (the others are at Martin, Vernhams Dean and Hawley). To find the exact spot follow the road named Hammer Vale along the valley of the river Wey to Hammer Bottom. The road crosses two arms of the river; a footpath to the left near the second bridge takes you to a footbridge (the first of two) where a mill once stood. Where the two arms of the river meet at this bridge is the junction of the three counties.

Two sluices and some masonry mark the site of the old ironworking mill. The site is known as Pophole and was first recorded in 1574 as a furnace named Pophall. Later it was classified as a forge and on Norden's 1604 map as a mill.

On the first road bridge the old cast-iron plate from its predecessor has been fixed; it reads: 'This bridge is insufficient to carry weights beyond ordinary traffic. By order. P D H B.' 'Ordinary traffic' then had a different meaning to what it has now!

As its name indicates Hammer Bottom was the scene of ironworking in days gone by at several mills in this valley. Waggoners Wells, the ponds on the east side of the parish, now a National Trust beauty spot, were probably once hammerponds for an ironworking mill further downstream. They were known as Wakeners Wells in the sixteenth century and the Ordnance Survey still describes them as 'Wakeners or Waggoners Wells'. (The National Trust adds an apostrophe for good measure – Waggoners' Wells.)

Sunken lanes are a conspicuous feature of the Bramshott area, more so than in any other part of the county; in some places the roadway is 20 ft below the top of the bank on either side. Bramshott is situated on the Hythe Beds, which consist of easily eroded sandstones. Gilbert White was one of the first to recognise the causes of sunken lanes–traffic over the ages and erosion by water. He remarked on their wild and grotesque appearance after floods or frost, enough to 'affright the ladies . . . and make timid horsemen shudder'. Downward erosion was brought to a halt by road metalling.

Woolmer Forest on the other hand is situated on the Folkestone Beds, which give rise to infertile heathlands. You can walk into Woolmer Forest (when the red warning flags are not up) from The Passfield Oak public house at Passfield Common. After crossing the Holly Water into the heart of the forest you will come to a ruined railway bridge and embankment, once part of the Longmoor Military Railway. This was a unique private railway; the Hollywater loop that crossed this bridge was used to train Royal Engineers in the construction and operation of a railway. The main part of the railway ran from Bordon to the army camp at Longmoor, and in 1933 an extension was completed to Liss on the Portsmouth to London line.

St Mary's churchyard has two special burial grounds, one for King George's Sanatorium for Sailors, the other for the Canadian soldiers who died at the camp on Bramshott Common (known as 'Mudsplosh' camp for obvious reasons) during the two world wars. Many of the Canadians died as a result of the influenza epidemic of 1917–18. Some were buried in St Joseph's Roman Catholic graveyard two miles north.

John Pym, who became the chief Parliamentary opponent of Charles I, was married in the church in 1604. The 200 church kneelers are each of a unique design, depicting the flora and fauna of the countryside around Bramshott.

Flora Thompson (see Grayshott) came to Liphook in 1916 and lived until 1927 at Ruskin House (now No. 6), London Road, which was then the post office (see plaque on the wall); her husband was the postmaster. There is a memorial bust of her outside the present post office.

Breamore

━ Breamore House and St Mary's Saxon church are well known and are visited by thousands of people every year, not many of whom stop in the village to see what else there is of interest. Between the Wiltshire border and Fordingbridge the river Avon meanders in great curves from side to side of its flood-plain, and at Breamore an 18th-century mill and a three-arched bridge stand astride the river.

Upstream from the mill, in the field by the river known as Priory Meadow, was St Michael's Priory. The site can be reached by a lane that crosses the course of the old Salisbury and Dorset Junction Railway (disused since 1964). Three stone coffins lie on the site of the burial ground of the priory; how old they are it is hard to say, but the priory was dissolved in 1536. These three lonely graves on the riverside, the only relics of a once-thriving community, are rather an eerie sight.

On the main road the old village stocks, or what is left of them, have been preserved. Most villages once had them, but few have survived (see Odiham). Note the three fire marks on the cottage named Japonica, one of the Norwich, one of the Sun and one other. The owners obviously thought that if they insured with three companies there was a chance of at least one fire-engine reaching them in time. But if they all had to come from Salisbury that was far from certain.

Breamore Marsh, between the main road and Upper Street, is just what the name implies – a boggy marshland crossed by footpaths. It is apparently a surviving manorial green still in use for grazing; cottage owners may each put out two geese and one gander! The grassland flora is of limited interest but the ponds are rich in aquatic flora.

How many visitors to Breamore House walk on through Breamore Wood to the Mizmaze on Breamore Down? It is a long uphill walk (1¼ miles) but a pleasant one. The date of the Mizmaze, one of the only two turf mazes in Hampshire, is not known but it is probably medieval. Turf mazes are found only in England and perhaps correspond to the inlaid stone or tile mazes and labyrinths that are found mainly in Continental churches. This however would imply an ecclesiastical origin for which there is no firm evidence. But whatever the purpose of their construction, mazes have been used since Tudor times for recreation; Shakespeare refers to them in two of his plays. The maze at Breamore is circular and is similar in design to those in Chartres Cathedral, Lucca Cathedral and Bayeux Abbey.

Brockenhurst

➤ William Gilpin, in his book *Remarks on Forest Scenery* (1791), wrote that 'Brokenhurst is a pleasant forest-village, lying in a bottom, adorned with lawns, groves and rivulets, and surrounded on the higher grounds by vast woods. – From the church-yard an expanded view opens over the whole.'

The lawns, groves and rivulets are still there, and away from the main road and shopping centre it remains a pleasant enough village; the view from the churchyard is still quite extensive. The railway came in 1847 and since then development has been almost entirely north of it, thus preserving the rural nature of the southern half of the village.

The old Bat and Ball inn suffered from engine smoke, so the Morant Arms that replaced it was built further away from the track. The original crossing-keeper's house stands near the main road level crossing. The Snakecatcher (formerly The Railway Inn) is named after 'Brusher' Mills, a local character who earned his living by catching snakes in the forest and selling them to London Zoo for one shilling each. His gravestone in the churchyard depicts the forest hut where he lived. Also in the churchyard are the graves of 94 New Zealand soldiers who died at hospitals here in the First World War.

A short walk across Setley Plain, south of Brockenhurst, parallel with and east of the Lymington branch railway line, will take you to a well-preserved pair of Bronze Age disc barrows (shown as 'Tumuli' on the Ordnance Survey map). They are unusual in that they overlap each other, the outer bank of the earlier northern barrow having been partly destroyed by the later one.

The Rhinefield Ornamental Drive, planted in 1859, is popular with motorists and walkers. Of the many different trees to be seen, four are the tallest of their species in Great Britain – a redwood, black spruce, red spruce and Spanish fir. They are exceeded in height however by a Wellingtonia that reaches 165 ft.

The regulations governing behaviour by the public in the New Forest are many and varied, but they are all designed to protect the forest and its flora and fauna. As well as more obvious prohibitions, you must not enter any mines in the forest, set up beehives, operate a hot-air balloon or a raft, or deliver a sermon. Preachers arriving by balloon and setting up beehives in a mine are definitely unwelcome! The regulation most often broken however is probably the speed limit of 20 mph.

The Naked Man is the six-foot-high stump of an aged oak tree standing by the side of the old Lymington to Ringwood road near Wilverley Post. It is shown on Taylor's map of 1759 as Wilverly Oak, and the hanging of smugglers is said to have taken place there.

Broughton

There were once about 25,000 dovecots or pigeon-houses in England, yet strangely relatively few have survived. In the Middle Ages pigeon meat was an important addition to the winter diet of the lucky owner of a dovecot, usually the lord of the manor. The dovecot was as important as the deer-park, the fishpond and the rabbit warren, but what the owner gained was lost by his tenants and neighbours because the pigeons fed on everybody's crops. Young birds were hatched every six weeks and provided a constant supply of meat. In the 18th century cattle began to be fed in winter on turnips, and pigeon meat became less important.

The brick dovecot in Broughton churchyard, rebuilt in 1684, is circular, but dovecots were built in many shapes and sizes; this one could house 482 pairs of pigeons. A new revolving central post or potence has recently been fitted; this is one of the few dovecots with a potence open to the public in England.

The village well in High Street has been covered over and the wheel removed. An inscribed stone records that it was made in the drought of 1921 by John Fripp in memory of his son, killed at Loos in 1915. An inscription on the inside reads:

On parent knees a naked new born child
weeping thou satst while all around thee smiled.
So live, that smiling in thy last long sleep
Calm thou mayst smile while all around thee weep.
Sir Wm. Jones. from the Persian

In High Street is the former Dowse's Charity School, founded in 1601 and repaired in 1864. Thomas Dowse died a year later in 1602, according to his memorial in St Mary's church. In the churchyard is the tomb of Anne Steele (1717–78), a famous hymn-writer of her day. She wrote 144 hymns, 34 psalms and about 50 poems; her hymns were popular with Baptists. Her fiancé was drowned a few hours before their intended wedding. She was born at the house in Rookery Lane now named Grandfather's. Also buried here is William Ander-

Dovecot in Broughton churchyard

son, whose headstone tells us that he was a popular agriculturist who won prizes for superior breeds of cattle and wrote an essay on stacking corn in wet seasons.

The Baptist church in High Street was built in 1816 by Henry Steele for the Anabaptists; the date of 1655 on the building refers to the first meeting of the Baptists in the village. The first Baptist church in England was built at Spitalfields in London in 1612.

Houses in the village that recall former trades are The Old Plough, The Old Coach House, The Old Malt House, Post House and Old Market House, outside which medieval markets may have been held. The Manor of Broughton was granted a weekly market and a yearly fair in 1246.

Burghclere

➤ Burghclere seems to have been an important place in the Middle Ages. Its name means 'borough of Clere' (Clere was perhaps the old name of the river Enborne). In 1218 it was known as Novus Burgus de Clere and was the site of a market belonging to the Bishop of Winchester.

The scarp of the Hampshire downs, with the prominent summits of Ladle Hill and Beacon Hill, crosses the southern part of the parish; both hills are crowned by Iron Age hill-forts. The one on Ladle Hill is of special interest to archaeologists because it is a rare example of a half-completed hill-fort, where one can study the method of construction of these great prehistoric defensive camps. The easiest approach to it is from Watership Down to the east.

The fort on Beacon Hill, reached by a steep climb from the A34, has a single rampart and ditch following the contours; inside are several hut circles, the sites of Iron Age homes. In one corner is the grave of Lord Carnarvon of Highclere Castle, the discoverer of the Tomb of Tutankhamun.

If you stand on the railway bridge in the village and look at the overgrown and waterlogged course of the old Didcot, Newbury and Southampton Railway, abandoned in the early 1960s after a life of nearly 80 years, and then look at the traffic on the nearby A34, which runs roughly parallel to the old railway all the way to Winchester, you may wonder why money takes precedence over common sense.

A few yards along Spring Lane is the former Highclere station building, now an attractive private house with the old platforms nicely landscaped. The station, though over two miles from Highclere village, was presumably named Highclere because there was another station at Old Burghclere that had to be named Burghclere. The latter was at first named Sydmonton and is also now a private house. *The Ghost Train*, the last of the three films with that name, starring Arthur Askey, was made there in 1941.

Near the railway bridge are the Sandham Memorial chapel, with its well-known Stanley Spencer murals, the lovely old thatched Laburnham Cottage (1677), the Carpenters Arms, and Budd's Farm, where William Cobbett stayed in 1826 and in his *Rural Rides* wrote about Mr Budd's wheat and Swedish turnips.

All Saints church at Old Burghclere was disused from 1838 to 1861, by which time it was in a sorry state, with brambles and alders growing inside. (Services were held in the new church at Burghclere.) Perhaps it was lucky in a way for it thus escaped the worst of Victorian restoration. The pews are 17th century, perhaps even earlier, and there are three 17th-century brasses. The tragic memorial to Edward Herbert records that while Secretary of State at Athens 'he was captured by Greek brigands and after ten days detention during which the large Ransom demanded was in vain offered he was cruelly murdered in 1870 in his 33rd year'.

Buriton

➤ St Mary's church, the Manor House and the village pond with its willow trees combine to make a traditional English village picture, seen here to better effect than in most villages in Hampshire. The church is very large for such a small village but until 1886 it was also the parish church of Petersfield. It has one unusual structural feature – the piers supporting the tower arch rest on projecting stone 'tables'. Around the font there are old paving stones from London (from London Bridge as at Steep?).

The Manor House was the home of Edward Gibbon, author of *The Decline and Fall of the Roman Empire* (which was not written at Buriton). His father had converted the old mansion into what was then a modern and comfortable house. Its 18th-century dovecot can be seen from North Lane.

The building that is now Nos. 38–46 High Street was once the poorhouse (built 1791) and it is not difficult to imagine it then, a large forbidding place overlooking the nearby cottages. It was not of course one of the Union workhouses; they came into existence in 1834 (see Droxford).

The old London to Portsmouth coach road (turnpiked in 1710) followed more or less the same line as the modern A3. At Gravel Hill, south of the Queen Elizabeth Country Park Centre, the old road passes near Bottom Cottage, which was once an inn. It was probably the one referred to in Dickens' *Nicholas Nickleby*, when Nicholas and Smike, on their journey from London, 'turned off the path to the door of a roadside inn, yet twelve miles short of Portsmouth.' It is shown on the Ordnance Survey map of 1810 as the Bottom Inn; two road books of that time refer to it as the Gravel Hill Inn.

Bottom Cottage, Buriton

Burley

In 1863 John Wise described Burley as 'one of the most primitive of Forest hamlets'. There is nothing primitive about it today – it unashamedly caters for the tourist and tripper. Its shops include A Coven of Witches, The Sorcerer's Apprentice Gift Shop, Rainbow's End, Wishing Well Gifts, Odd Spot, Witchcraft, The Magpies' Nest, Goldilocks and The Burley Fudge Shop. If you like that sort of thing you will like Burley. The Manor Farm Tea Rooms claims to have been famous for its cream teas since 1904, when some of its customers must have arrived in carriages or early motor cars, and the less wealthy ones by bicycle or on foot. The Queens Head public house is worth a visit to see its collection of old hunting trophies.

Burley has a surfeit of milestones and commemorative stones. One of the milestones in the village, on the Lymington to Ringwood road, is inscribed 'Tho.Eyre H.Bromfield Surveyors 1802'. Thomas Eyre was a local benefactor, a remarkable but mysterious man. He is buried in the old chapel, which he partly paid for in 1789 and which was rebuilt in 1842–3.

He also erected two commemorative stones (one stands at Copse Corner and the other near the Queens Head) inscribed:

'Rest and be Thankful   Peace Restored 27th March 1802'.

This refers to the Treaty of Amiens, which brought a temporary stop to war in Europe. Unfortunately for Thomas Eyre his relief was short-lived, for it was not long before war broke out again. The stone near the Queens Head was known as the Bread Stone, because by the terms of his will charity was dispensed on the stone each year to twelve poor women and girls.

At a house near Castle Hill there is another stone erected by Thomas Eyre, with this incredible inscription:

Black Bush in the Vill of Bistern Closes
Near this is the remains of a camp or castle, either
of the ancient Britons, Romans or Saxons, with the
Agger, Vallum, Fosse, Tumulus, or Barrows.
Be civil, quiet, and useful. T. EYRE 1823

The camp referred to is on Castle Hill; it is in fact an Iron Age hill-fort, which his description does not really include! Thomas Eyre was apparently a man of estimable character, so his ignorance of archaeology can be forgiven. One of his favourite sayings was 'An hour lost in the morning is not so easily recovered'.

Bursledon

➤ In the days of wooden ships Bursledon was a flourishing shipbuilding centre. Daniel Defoe noted that two 80-gun ships had been launched from the shipyard there. In his book *Captain Singleton* Defoe wrote about Bursledon: 'and there I attended the carpenters, and such people as were employed in building a ship for the . . . Newfoundland trade.'

Two great local shipbuilders were Philemon Ewer (died in 1750), who built seven large warships, and George Parsons (1729–1812), who built the 74-gun HMS *Elephant*, Nelson's flagship at the Battle of Copenhagen. Both men have memorials in St Leonard's church. The memorial tablet to John Tayler on the exterior nave wall depicts brickmaking tools, a reminder of another once-important local industry.

In the old village of Bursledon there are now only two public houses, The Jolly Sailor, an 18th-century inn on the waterfront, and The Vine in High Street. There were once two or three more, including The New Inn (now Greywell) near the tiny village green, and The Dolphin, a splendid old timber-framed building with an upper-storeyed porch and an ornamental wrought-iron signboard bracket.

In School Road a little Gothic belfry surmounts the entrance to the Roman Catholic chapel of Our Lady of the Rosary (at the house named Greyladyes). The times of the services are embossed in stone on a much-weathered tablet – confessions are on Saturdays. The chapel was built by Mrs Shawe-Storey, who modernised several houses in the village.

Lands End Road ends at a tiny public hard and landing-place. Land's End House, on the site of yet another inn, has a 'stork' weather-vane, Parsons Plot commemorates George

Parsons the shipbuilder, Ewers was the home of Philemon Ewer, and the Elephant Boatyard is named after HMS *Elephant*.

Catherington

➤ Chalk downlands, of which Catherington Down is a fine example, are increasingly threatened by encroachment and erosion. The prominent strip lynchets here were the result of medieval cultivation on the steep hillside, when the soil turned downhill by the plough formed parallel banks (risers) and terraces (treads).

In All Saints churchyard the tomb of the Kean family (Charles Kean, his wife Eleonora and his mother Mary) has the inscription: 'Leaders of the English Theatre 1851–1859'. This refers to the plays, mainly Shakespeare and melodrama, produced at the Princess's Theatre in London by Kean. He was a serious and hard-working actor and manager, unlike his wayward genius of a father Edmund Kean. His wife was the actress Ellen Tree. His mother lived at Keydell House (now destroyed).

Also here, hidden in the corner of the churchyard, is the tomb of Admiral Sir Charles Napier (1786–1860). He had a long and varied career at sea, including the command of the Portuguese fleet; he lost a fortune promoting steamboat experiments on the river Seine. He lived at Merchistoun Hall, an 18th-century house with an imposing ground-floor colonnade, now used as the Horndean Community Centre.

Catherington House was the home of Admiral Samuel Hood (1724–1816), who was described by Nelson as 'the best officer that England has'.

Chalton

➤ Chalton has always been a very small village, but was almost certainly larger in the Middle Ages than it is now. Long before then there was a Romano-British village on Chalton Down; it was occupied from the first century AD to the fourth century AD. It was excavated in 1964–5 when many finds were made, including evidence of both timber and masonry buildings. The site is an unploughed field at the summit of the steep slope above the Buriton–Havant road, adjacent to the southern boundary of Holt Down Plantation (a public footpath passes it).

This minor road from Buriton to Havant was the favoured route from London to Portsmouth in the 17th century, before the road past Butser Hill became in 1710 one of the earliest turnpikes in England, and it continued in use in the 18th century. In his *Britannia* (1675) John Ogilby took the Butser route for his survey, but also marked the Buriton turning a mile south of Petersfield as 'to Havant & to Portsmouth by Buriton'. It is significant that the railway opened in 1859 follows this old route very closely.

The Red Lion is one of the oldest and one of the most picturesque inns in Hampshire. It is thatched with the outer parts of its upper storey oversailing and the middle part recessed behind brackets, a common arrangement in old Wealden public houses. St Michael's church opposite has a notable east window, a fine example of the Geometrical Decorated style. The churchyard gate has a notice: 'Sheep at work'; the churchyard is often full of grazing sheep – to save on mowing expenses!

Chawton

 Chawton is a relatively quiet backwater now; years ago traffic on the A31 thundered down the village street and round the corner by Jane Austen's House. Other interesting houses include Bay Tree Cottage, with a Royal Arms on its wall, The Old Post Office, a tiny cottage set well back by the name of Nr Old Post Office, and Clinkers (c.1550) with its medallions of Rubens and Shakespeare, which were probably made at Chawton Forge next door.

In St Nicholas's churchyard are the graves of Jane Austen's sister Cassandra and their mother, also named Cassandra. Most of the memorials in the church are to the Knight family. Others include the Reverend John Hinton, who was rector for 58 years (1744–1802), and Sir Edward Bradford, Metropolitan Police Commissioner.

Cheriton

In 1822 William Cobbett described Cheriton as 'a little, hard, iron village, where all seems to be as old as the hills that surround it.' Whatever he meant then by 'hard' and 'iron', there is nothing hard about Cheriton today; the old cottages in the main street and on 'The Island', with the infant Itchen flowing past, contribute to a scene as pleasant as any in Hampshire.

St Michael's church stands on what is thought to be a prehistoric burial mound. That is quite possible, for in Saxon times some churches were built on pagan religious sites and burial places in order to affirm the supremacy of Christianity over heathen gods, and continuity of religion was maintained because churches were usually rebuilt on the same sites as their predecessors.

Between the years 1348 and 1351 there were five changes of vicar, a salutary reminder of the terrible onslaught of the Black Death and its aftermath. The village was almost depopulated, 25 families having been wiped out.

The name Brandy Mount recalls the prevalence of smuggling in the 18th and 19th centuries, Cheriton being well known for its illicit trade in Hollands brandy. Even one of the curates and his bell-ringers were involved in smuggling. The Flowerpots public house is not all that old; though the name is unusual now, it was a common sign in old London.

The memorial to the Battle of Cheriton, the last battle ever fought in Hampshire, is situated at a road junction a mile north of the main battle site, which was near Cheriton Wood. The memorial is not even in the parish of Cheriton! Perhaps the village is reluctant to be associated with what was a decisive battle of the Civil War.

Truffles are underground fungi, highly esteemed as delicacies. They occur near beech trees on chalk slopes and were once hunted by specially-trained dogs. In the 19th century and early 20th century truffle-hunting supported six families in Cheriton, which is thought to have been the last place in England where truffle-hunting was carried on in such a big way. The pastime seems to have almost died out in England now. Gilbert White of Selborne recalled meeting a truffle-hunter, who asked 2/6d a pound for them (when bread was 2d a pound, meat was 4d a pound and a labourer's wages were 8/- a week).

Chilbolton

Chilbolton Common, which can be reached by footpath from the village or over the Test from Wherwell, is of exceptional scientific interest. It has never been ploughed or treated with chemicals and is grazed by cattle. Its banks and ditches produce an alternation of chalk-loving plants (eg fairy flax) and chalk-hating plants (eg tormentil). Over 110 species are regularly recorded here by naturalists and scientists. It is a delightful spot that evokes memories of peaceful days long gone elsewhere.

Electricity came to Chilbolton only in 1933. The villagers are said to have been reluctant to have it, fearing that they would be blown up, so they were bribed with free lights and fittings.

A custom peculiar to Chilbolton was the baking of mid-Lent wafers; though the precise origin is uncertain, the custom is thought to date back to pre-Reformation days. The wafers were baked in a pair of tongs that imprinted a design on one side and the letters 'I.S.' on the other.

Chilcomb

At the end of a narrow lane, with the chalk downland of Deacon Hill towering above it, is the little parish church of St Andrew. It is less than two miles as the crow flies from the centre of Winchester, yet on a quiet day (when the nearby army firing range is silent) it seems to be miles from anywhere. It is early Norman in date, so early that Saxon influence is evident, for the nave is high relative to its length and the chancel arch, which has rough zigzag ornament, is quite narrow.

In AD 636 the manor of Chilcomb was given by King Cynegils to the Church in Winchester and it remained in their possession until about 1893. A copy of the charter signed by Edward the Elder confirming this gift is in the church. The remarkable thing about the manor of Chilcomb was its size; it covered about 15 square miles around Winchester. Its origin is still unexplained. Domesday Book mentions nine churches in Chilcomb, which were probably those at Compton, Hursley, Weeke, Chilcomb, Littleton, Sparsholt and Morestead, St Catherine on the hill and the White Monastery.

John Washington, vicar from 1803 to 1812, was a direct descendant of Robert de Washington, an ancestor of George Washington. At that time the only male representatives of the family were the vicar and his sons.

The Hospital of St Mary Magdalen stood near the Winchester to Alresford road on what is now called Morn Hill. It was founded some time before 1158 for the care of lepers, probably by Bishop Henry de Blois who founded St Cross Hospital in Winchester.

Disaster struck the hospital twice in the 17th century. During the Civil War Royalist troops killed many of the sheep, stole the corn and burnt all the woodwork, including the altar table in the chapel. Then in 1665 the Government evicted the inmates in order to house Dutch prisoners of war, who inflicted even more damage than the Royalists. The buildings were finally demolished in 1788; the Norman chapel doorway was incorporated in St Peter's Roman Catholic church in Winchester, and other materials were used in the building of Rosemary Close, Water Lane.

Chilton Candover

➤ A chance remark to the vicar in 1927 set him thinking. An old man in the village had said that as a boy he used to 'go down under the old church and kick skulls around'. The vicar started to excavate the site of the medieval church, which had been pulled down in 1878. To his astonishment he found the crypt of a Norman church, forgotten about for 50 years until the old man's remark.

The Norman Crypt at Chilton Candover

The crypt consists of an apse and a tunnel-vaulted room separated by a narrow round-headed archway. The walls are four feet thick, with tiny windows set just above ground level; inside are ancient coffin-lids and a Norman font. Crypts are usually associated with cathedrals and other large churches, but many smaller churches had them, though few of the Norman period have survived, which makes this find all the more remarkable.

In the field that you have to cross to get to the crypt there are terraces and hollow-ways that indicate the site of the medieval village. In 1562 a man named John Fisher bought the manor and proceeded to destroy the entire village with the exception of the church and one farm. The inhabitants were presumably left to fend for themselves.

Across the B3046 a magnificent avenue of yew trees, over half a mile long and perhaps the longest in England, runs uphill as far as the back road to Alresford. William Cobbett wrote of these trees that 'they have probably been a century or two in growing' and that 'the yew will last as long as the timber of any other tree that we grow in England'.

Avenues of trees first became fashionable in the early 17th century, as a formal approach to the new country houses that were being built everywhere; they became even more popular as the century progressed. It is not known when this avenue was planted, but it is said that it led up to a house that was demolished in the 18th century. No house was shown on Taylor's map of 1759, but not far away was the Bangor Inn, which almost certainly derived its name from the Welsh drovers who passed that way with their flocks of sheep. The Woolpack Inn at Totford must have got its name in a similar way.

Colemore

➤ The little Norman church of St Peter ad Vincula is officially redundant but services are occasionally held there. Two grave-stones in the chancel provide an extraordinary coincidence.

That of Richard Pocock (should be Pococke) states that he died in 1718 at the age of 83 after having been rector for 59 years, and that of James Cookson states that he died in 1835 also at the age of 83, and also after having been rector for 59 years.

To be exact Pococke was rector for 59 years and 3 months and Cookson for 58 years and 8 months, but what a coincidence! Pococke died in fact in 1719 – the error on his gravestone arose because of confusion over the new calendar (see Basing). He was, according to the inscription, a man of singular probity, eminent piety and great charity. (He was also a widower for 44 years.) His grandson, Richard Pococke, was a famous traveller in the East.

Cookson, described elsewhere as a man of genial disposition, wrote a book or tract entitled *Thoughts on Polygamy*, after which he got married! The record for the longest Church of England incumbency is held by the Reverend Bartholomew Edwards, who was rector of St Nicholas, Ashill, Norfolk, for 75 years and 357 days between 1813 and 1889.

Compton and Shawford

Compton adjoins the city of Winchester but is still separated from it by green fields and water-meadows. The name means 'village in a combe' and Compton is just that, a long street on the side of a dry chalk valley.

All Saints church is unusual in having two naves and two chancels, the Norman nave and chancel serving as north aisle and chapel respectively since the new nave and chancel were built in 1905. The old and the new have been very well integrated.

John Barton (no relation as far as is known!) was vicar from 1677 to 1683. He started the parish register of burials and also recorded the collections for charities. For the rebuilding of St Paul's Cathedral £1.18s.1d was collected. The local people must have been generous or wealthy because they also gave money for the redemption of English prisoners in Algiers, for distressed churches in Poland and for poor Protestants from France.

All Saints School near the church dates partly from 1838 when attendance was voluntary. Its full name was 'Church of England Voluntary School for the Education of the Labouring Poorer Classes'.

The Shawford viaduct may soon be incorporated into the M3 motorway but until then it remains the longest railway viaduct in Hampshire, 2,014 ft long and 40 ft high. The Didcot, Newbury and Southampton line joined the main line just south of the viaduct, and was in operation from 1891 to 1966. The line was originally intended to reach Southampton via Twyford and Chilworth but for financial reasons it was decided to link it to the main line at Shawford Junction.

Shawford Down is a public open space and a convenient starting-point for walks in either direction along the Itchen Navigation and to Comptom and Twyford villages. We tend to think of the present time as the heyday of golf, but in 1900 there were two courses in Compton, both long since gone, one on Shawford Down and the other on Compton Down.

On the down there are two war memorials. The one nearest the bypass (known as the Wayside Cross) commemorates the dead of the First World War; it formerly stood where soldiers had their first rest when marching from Winchester to Southampton. The larger memorial commemorates the Second World War dead; a stone has been thoughtfully placed near it inscribed 'Write on this not on our war memorial'.

Corhampton

➤ Corhampton and Meonstoke form a single parish, the river Meon separating one village from the other. Corhampton, the smaller of the two, has by far the older church. It was built in the early 11th century and is a remarkable survival of a small Saxon village church, almost complete and very little altered.

The nave, chancel arch and north doorway are original, and typical Saxon features are the 'long-and-short' stones at the wall corners and the pilaster strips on the walls. The Saxon sundial on the south wall is divided into eight sections, not twelve as it would be today. This is because the Saxons divided the day and night into eight three-hour 'tides' and not into 24 hours. The incised lines on their sundials mark the middle point of each 'tide', but on the mass-dials or scratch-dials introduced by the Normans the lines indicate the hours. On a sundial the line marking noon is correct throughout the year (if the dial faces due south) but the lines marking the other hours are not accurate in winter.

The wall-paintings in the chancel are among the earliest and most important in Hampshire; they date probably from the 12th century. A Romano-British coffin, now used as a flower-bed, is in the churchyard, which also has one of the largest yew trees in the county.

Crawley

➤ It is hard to believe that Crawley, today one of the most attractive and well-kept villages in Hampshire, in 1900 was described as dilapidated and unattractive, a nondescript place with an unpaved road and broken-down barns and cottages.

The change in Crawley's fortunes came with the move to Crawley Court in 1901 of Ernest Philippi, a Glasgow business man. He created a model village by buying all properties that came up for sale, rebuilding some, renovating others. He even made his gardeners responsible for the cottage gardens front-ing the village street.

The maturing of trees and shrubs in the village over the last 50 years has offset the once-conspicuous mock-Tudor style of many of the houses and has resulted in the present attractive appearance of Crawley, assisted by restrictive covenants that have kept out all commercial premises except one public house.

There was a church here in 1086, when the bishop himself was lord of the manor. The unusual feature of St Mary's, the present church, is the nave arcade, possibly 15th century, which is constructed of wooden posts with arched braces and tie-beams. The use of wood for the pillars, though not unique, is very rare.

In the churchyard is Archdeacon Jacob's post, which once stood on the Andover road. It seems that the Archdeacon, who was the vicar at the time, lost his way home one winter's evening, so he erected this post and hung a lantern on it whenever he went that way. He was the vicar from 1831 to 1884 and during that time no less than 18 assistant curates served under him. This was no reflection on the Archdeacon for he was apparently well-thought-of in the village.

A memorial tablet in the church records the death in 1811 of John Jarrett, aged 34, in Madeira, where he had gone to recover his health!

Crondall

➤ Crondall is as attractive a village as any you will find in Hampshire. The Borough in particular, in the centre of the village, has several fine old cottages including Old Meeting House (formerly the meeting-house of the Plymouth Brethren), dating from the mid-16th century, and Chapel Cottage adjoining it. The Plume of Feathers public house opposite has an oversailing upper storey and is the oldest inn in the parish.

There are several curious things in All Saints church, including two coffin trolleys, a chest of 1546 and an anchorite's cell. The brass in the chancel floor to Nicholas de Caerwent, who died in 1381, is one of the three oldest in the county.

A brass plate in the south transept depicts a skeleton in a shroud, with the inscription:

> John Eager, des March the XX, 1641 –
> You earthly impes which here behold
> This picture with your eyes
> Remember the end of mortal men
> And where their glory lies
> I.E.

This naturally enough is known as the 'Imp' memorial. John Eager, or Eggar, founded the grammar school at Alton. The memorial to Deborah Maxwell states that she 'died by her dress catching fire whilst her attention was engaged in writing'.

The massive brick church tower of 1659 was modelled on the tower of a church at Battersea. Turning to less tangible things, the ghost of a Roundhead soldier on horseback is said to have been seen riding up the avenue and disappearing through the church doorway.

Heath Lane leads uphill from the village to Warren Corner at the junction of Dora's Green Lane, a spot known as Queen's View because Queen Victoria is said to have gone there several times in order to admire the view to the west. She is supposed to have been driven over from Aldershot after inspecting the troops and who can blame her for getting away from that? In the small thicket at the crossroads you will find a well-preserved brick hexagonal pill-box, one of the relics of the special defensive line that was erected across the country in 1940.

Crookham Village

➤ The Basingstoke Canal meanders through the parish, and the site of Crookham wharf has been made into a car-park, a convenient starting-point for a walk along the tow-path. Canal Cottage, near the old wharf, was the home of Mark Hicks, who worked for the canal company for 82 years. His name went into *The Guinness Book of Records* as the man with the longest working career in one job in Great Britain, but it was there for only a short time – his record has now been superseded. He started work at the age of ten and was working as canal bailiff four days before his death in 1966 at the age of 92.

The 37-mile-long canal had 29 locks, 69 bridges, two aqueducts and a tunnel. It brought coal and manufactured goods to Hampshire and took timber, grain and malt to London. The canal was derelict for many years; restoration commenced in 1973 and now after years of digging and dredging much of it is navigable again.

Crux Easton

➤ Geoffrey de Havilland, the well-known aircraft designer and manufacturer, lived here; his father was the vicar. He built his first aircraft at Highclere and made his first flight from Beacon Hill in 1909; later he took local people for flights. A less welcome though temporary resident was Sir Oswald Mosley, founder of the British Union of Fascists, who was interned at Crux Easton during the Second World War.

The name Crux derives from Croc the huntsman, who held the manor in 1086 and may have been warden of Chute Forest. Later the manor came into the possession of the Lisle family, one of whom, Edward Lisle, wrote a best-selling book on agriculture entitled *Observations in Husbandry*, published in 1757 more than 30 years after his death. He had 20 children; his daughters built a grotto in what is now Grotto Copse and Alexander Pope, a friend of the family, wrote a poem about it.

INSCRIPTION ON A GROTTO, THE WORK OF NINE
LADIES
Here, shunning idleness at once and praise,
This radiant pile nine rural sisters raise;
The glitt'ring emblem of each spotless dame,
Clear as her soul and shining as her frame;
Beauty which nature only can impart,
And such a polish as disgraces art;
But fate disposed them in this humble sort,
And hid in deserts what would charm a court.

He also wrote a poem about the sisters.

Authors the world and their dull brains have traced,
To fix the ground where Paradise was placed.
Mind not their learned whims and idle talk,
Here, here's the place, where these bright angels walk.

The house opposite the church, built in 1847, was once the village school. Twenty-three of its pupils came from the row of cottages on the Woodcott road that is now named Field House but was then for some reason named The City. The house named Three Legged Cross at the junction of the Newbury road with the Ox Drove has a curious sign on the front; it was once an inn, perhaps even when drovers passed that way.

St Michael's church is a textbook example of a small Georgian village church. It was built in 1775 and has its original font, lectern and pulpit. There are said to be tunnels under the village connecting the church, the old rectory, the manor house and the former school. None of these tunnels have been seen for a long time and their purpose remains a mystery.

Curdridge

➤ At the side of the Victorian drinking-fountain near Botley station there is a memorial with this inscription: 'This Stone is Erected to Perpetuate a Most Cruel Murder Committed on the Body of Thomas Webb a Poor Inhabitant of Swanmore on the 11th of February 1800 by John Diggins a Private Soldier In the Talbot Fencibles Whose remains are Gibbeted on the adjoining Common'.

There are two mistakes on the memorial; 'Talbot' should be 'Tarbert' and 'Diggins' should be 'Diggon'. Fencibles (short for Defensibles) were volunteer soldiers raised and paid by patriotic bodies or wealthy men, a sort of Home Guard of the time. This particular regiment was formed in Tarbert, county Kerry, Ireland.

The full story was reported in the *Hampshire Chronicle*. Thomas Webb, described as a 'poor old travelling man', was met by two soldiers who robbed him of a few shillings, stabbed him and threw him into a ditch. Covered in blood he managed to reach the house of Mr Daniel Barfoot a mile away, where a surgeon was sent for. Webb died soon afterwards but not before giving particulars of his attackers.

As a result three soldiers from Botley barracks were taken into custody and charged with murder. At the trial two were discharged for lack of evidence and Diggon was sentenced to be hanged, though he was not the one who inflicted the fatal wound. Several other men were on trial at the same assizes for various acts of thieving and house-breaking. Though no violence was involved they were all sentenced to death, but most of them were later reprieved. When the act of theft brought a death sentence anyway, it is not surprising that the person robbed was often killed if the only witness.

On 10th March, only a month after the murder, Diggon was executed on a gallows and his body taken to Curdridge Common to be hung in chains on the gibbet, the position of which is marked on the Ordnance Survey map of 1810.

Damerham

➤ The manor of Damerham belonged to Glastonbury Abbey in the Middle Ages; the tithe barn where produce was collected for handing over to the abbey still exists at Court Farm.

The church is dedicated to St George, one of the very few of this dedication in Hampshire, though it is fairly common in England as a whole. Over the south doorway is a carving of St George killing a Saracen at the Battle of Antioch in 1098 during the First Crusade; it is probably of Norman date as the shape of the horse is similar to that in other Norman carvings. It was discovered in 1916 embedded in the wall of the old vicarage.

The massive Norman tower stands at the south-east corner of the nave, a most unusual position. The nave, chancel and porch have wagon-roofs, a feature of this area (Martin and Rockbourne churches also have them), though they are more common in the south-west than in the south-east of England. An ancient preaching cross stands in the churchyard.

The row of houses opposite The Compasses public house now known as The Terrace and formerly as The Barracks was built as temporary accommodation for the villagers after a disastrous fire in 1863. The houses though temporary were so solidly built that they will stand for many years yet. The only discordant building in the village is the ghastly corrugated-iron village hall.

Pillar-box at Denmead

Denmead

➤ Standing by the roadside at Worlds End is one of the 23 survivors of the first National Standard pillar-boxes, made by Messrs Cochrane & Co of Dudley between 1859 and 1866. This one is dated 1859 and is the second oldest pillar-box in Hampshire (see Milford on Sea), in its bright red paint looking just like new.

The design, to meet the demand for a standard type of pillar-box throughout the country, was the result of the combined ideas of the Controllers of the London Districts and the Birmingham Surveyor. Note the small posting aperture with its flap for protection against rain.

The 1873 Ordnance Survey 1/2500-scale map does not show this pillar box so it must have been moved here from another location at some time between 1873 and 1903, when it is noted in *Kelly's Directory*.

Denny Lodge

➤ Denny Lodge is included in this book because it is the largest parish in Hampshire (25.6 square miles). Though it has no church, no school and no public hall, it does have a railway station (Beaulieu Road) and four public houses, one of them appropriately named The Bold Forester, because the whole of the parish except a small area on the north-east falls within the New Forest.

The Bishop's Dyke is a four-mile-long bank enclosing an area of marshy ground known as the Bishop of Winchester's Purlieu, and is shown on the Ordnance Survey map. Its eastern extremity is within a short distance of the car parks at Pig Bush and Beaulieu Road Station. The Bishop's Dyke and its enclosure is one of the most puzzling enigmas in the county.

According to legend one of the Bishops of Winchester was granted as much land as he could crawl around in a day, and in the event he managed over four miles. The historical fact is that in 1284 King Edward I granted the Bishop of Winchester 500 acres of land in the New Forest (the Dyke encloses about 400 acres). The enclosure remained Church property until 1942. The enigma is why the Bishop chose (by crawling or otherwise) an area which even then must have been bog, in preference to an area of woodland or heathland that would have been much more useful for grazing or hunting. We shall probably never know.

Droxford

► Many of the houses in Droxford are Georgian and a few are even earlier. They are built mostly of local bricks with roofs of local tiles; there are not many thatched cottages, which are more common on the chalklands. Noteworthy are The Manor House (17th century), Sarum House and the White Horse Inn (both 18th century), and the County Police Station (1858), still used by the police. At the north end of the main street Old Post House, Old Bakery, Brewery Cottage and The Malt House are reminders of shops and trades of former years.

The Droxford workhouse, or 'Union' as it was called, was built in 1837 and served eleven villages in this area. The Unions (there were about 25 in Hampshire) were built to replace the parish workhouses and the one at Droxford was probably a typical example. A staff of four looked after 200 inmates who were given work, food and shelter as an alternative to starvation. The men spent ten hours a day picking oakum or crushing bones for use as fertilizer; the women worked in the kitchen or in the laundry. Breakfast was bread and gruel, dinner and supper bread and cheese. Until about 1842 husbands and wives, and parents and children, were kept strictly apart and talking at meals was forbidden.

As well as able-bodied people the workhouse inmates included young, old, sick and mad people, cripples and tramps. Only those in despair or near starvation would voluntarily enter a workhouse. Once inside most people were afraid to leave, though they were quite free to do so. The prevailing idea held by the authorities was that poverty was the result of bad character and not of misfortune, and that idleness must be punished by starvation. Therefore the workhouse, to be effective, as far as possible had to resemble a prison. The trouble was that conditions designed to deter the able-bodied were applied to children, the old, and the sick. The Droxford Union, which stood on the corner of Union Lane and North End Lane, was demolished in 1971, the last local reminder of man's inhumanity to man.

Izaak Walton, author of *The Compleat Angler* and fisherman *par excellence*, often came to Droxford to visit his son-in-law, who was the rector. He considered the river Meon the best in England for trout.

The parish church has two curious features, dormer windows in the nave roof, inserted in the 19th century in order to brighten the interior, and an odd-looking square stair-turret in the tower, unique in Hampshire.

(Droxford station – see Soberton.)

Dummer

➤ Dummer was once known as Dunmere, 'the lake or mere on a hill'. There is no mere now, nor can one imagine where it could have been on these chalklands. Dummer is a pleasantly attractive village, if you ignore the modern houses at the north end. Old trades have died out, as is seen by houses named The Old Forge, The Old Brewery and Foundry House, to be replaced by the new trade of catering for visitors and tourists, in the Chapel House Gallery with its prints and crafts.

The village street is divided into Up Street and Down Street, and you can't make any mistakes with that! Near The Queen Inn is the tile-roofed village well erected in 1897. The well-shaft has been covered over but the extraordinary ten-foot-diameter wooden tread-wheel survives; one person operated the wheel while another worked the brake and removed the bucket.

The real treasure of Dummer is All Saints church, with its ancient pulpit, gallery and rood canopy. The gallery extends over half the length of the nave because the latter is so small. The rood canopy above the chancel arch is a very rare survival, certainly unique in Hampshire. Not many roods had canopies and few of them have survived. No medieval roods survived their official destruction in the 16th century.

Pulpits were used in monasteries long before they were used in parish churches (see Beaulieu). The earliest wooden pulpits to have survived are of the late 14th century, and the one at Dummer of about 1380 is one of the six oldest in England. Preachers have used this pulpit for over 600 years; one who did so was the eloquent George Whitefield, who became well-known in England. At first a follower of the Wesleys, he later went his own way and helped to found the Calvinist Methodists.

Generations of the same families have sat here, listening to the man in the pulpit and saying their prayers; this little church reminds us of the continuity of English life and religion. A charity board records a bequest in 1610 to provide a small house and garden to be used for the instruction of six boys. This was the foundation of Dummer school, which was on the north side of Up Street. It continued for 361 years until its abrupt closure by the education authority in 1971.

The Diaries of Dummer, by A. M. W. Stirling, published in 1934, is a highly interesting account of the diaries kept by Stephen Terry (1774–1867) of Dummer House. It presents a vivid picture of the life of a country gentleman in a small village.

East Dean

➤ The Southampton and Salisbury Canal utilised the Andover Canal from Redbridge as far as Kimbridge, then followed a course through Lockerley and East Dean towards Salisbury, but it was never completed beyond Alderbury. This western arm from Kimbridge to Alderbury was in use for only a few years, from about 1802 to 1806, before the company became bankrupt. The canal never attracted much trade and the enterprise proved a disaster.

The remains of one of the canal locks can be seen on the west side of a bridge on the road between Lockerley and Holbury Wood, about 100 yards south of the bridge over the river Dun. The south side of the lock wall is 35 ft long and 5 ft high. The canal bed survives here and at several places between Lockerley and West Dean.

St Winfrid's is a little gem of a church. The nave walls are probably of Norman date but there are no details earlier than the 13th-century east window. Everything inside the church is mercifully unrestored, from the old timber-framed doorway to the roughly-fashioned tie-beam rafters, the old benches and the tiny 17th-century gallery. Note the nail-studded door, a relic of the days when the clerk or churchwarden paid a few pence each for rats and other vermin and nailed them to the door.

East Meon

➤ The river Meon rises only a mile south of East Meon and flows gently through High Street; years ago before improvements to the bridges there were periodic floods in the streets. Looking along Church Street from The George inn there is a dramatic view of All Saints church with Park Hill towering above it.

The first village school was held in the north transept of the church until a proper school was opened; this first school is the house named Windwhistle on the road to Langrish and is dated 1839. The day school and the Sunday school both used the church, and an observer in 1816 noted that 160 children attended on Sundays. (The population of East Meon in 1811 was about 1,150.) Probably not so many attended on weekdays because they were excused if they were working and school was not compulsory anyway.

All Saints church is one of the best Norman churches in the south of England. It has one of the seven black Tournai marble fonts in the country; the wonderful carvings on it include the Creation of Adam, the Expulsion from Paradise, and dogs chasing doves (the wicked persecuting the faithful). The pulpit of 1706 was brought from Holy Trinity, Minories, a church that once stood near the Tower of London; the original stone pulpit disappeared at the time of the church restoration in 1870.

In the east wall of the south transept there is a stone with the words 'Amens Plenty'. In its original place on the floor it covered the grave of four men buried in an upright position; they were said to be Parliamentary soldiers killed in the village. A more prominent memorial to dead soldiers is the stained glass in the east window, which depicts the patron saints of all the Allied countries in the First World War.

On the wall of Giants Cottage at Oxenbourne, east of East Meon, a grotesque face greets the passer-by. Somebody with an eccentric sense of humour has arranged stones and flints to form the features of a human face, hence the name of the cottage.

East Meon pest house, in Ramsdean Road, Stroud, was built in 1703 according to its stone inscription. It was probably used alternately as a pest house and a poorhouse until the Union workhouse was built at Petersfield. When it was built the pest house was as far from the village as possible but within the parish (it is now in Petersfield). Many towns and villages had a pest house at that time to house those with infectious diseases (see Odiham).

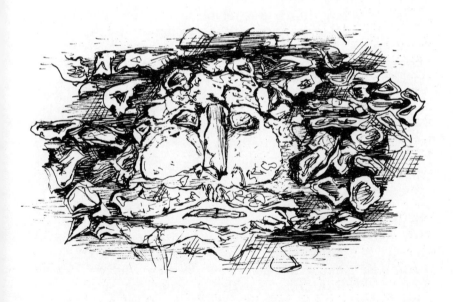

Detail of Giants Cottage, East Meon

East Woodhay

➤ The parish of East Woodhay consists of separate hamlets, scattered over a wide area, with names such as North End, East End, Gore End and Ball Hill; they probably originated as clearings in the forest that once covered this region.

Pilot Hill, the highest point in Hampshire (937 ft above sea-level), is just within the parish, only 200 yards from the county boundary. Until the parish of Combe was transferred to Berkshire in 1895 the highest point in Hampshire was Walbury Hill. You can walk to Pilot Hill (and on to Walbury Hill) by an ancient track known as the Ox Drove, which crosses the road from Ashmansworth to East Woodhay church. From this old track there are superb views of the Berkshire vale. The Ox Drove was one of the roads along which sheep and cattle were taken to and from the markets of south-east England. Sheep were penned for the night at Post Office Farm in East Woodhay and cattle likewise at East End.

East Woodhay church was rebuilt in 1823 and is unmistakably late Georgian, even though the Victorians did their worst by inserting Decorated-style windows. It is dedicated to St Martin of Tours, the saint who supposedly gave half of his cloak to a beggar. The restrained and impressive monument to Edward Goddard and his wife, which depicts them in their everyday clothes, is a fitting memorial to a man of 'sober life and conversation'. Many good people lived here, if we are to believe their memorial inscriptions. John Bailey was 'Social, Honest,Pious', and Edward Wimbolt, a chirurgeon (the old name for surgeon), had two wives (in succession, not at the same time) both of exemplary character, lucky fellow! Bishop Ken, who refused to let Nell Gwyn into his house, was once the rector here.

Curious names abound in East Woodhay; Gore End, Broad Layings, Blindman's Gate (where a blind man was in charge of a turnpike gate), and Bat's Grave (a man named Bat who committed suicide and was buried, as were most suicides, at a crossroads).

The Herb Garden at Hollington, in a 19th-century walled garden, displays for sale an extraordinary variety of herbs, also roses and fruit trees. Its formal culinary garden won a Gold Medal at the Chelsea Flower Show.

Eling

➤ The only surviving medieval toll in Hampshire has to be paid by owners of vehicles that cross the Bartley Water at Eling tide-mill. The causeway replaced a succession of bridges; the toll has been paid since at least 1418, the date of the earliest known lease. The mill and toll were owned by Winchester College until 1975, when they were given to the local Council, and the tenancy of the mill has always included the right to charge a toll. The toll charge in 1418 is not known but in 1800 it was six pence for a four-wheeled carriage and in 1967 it was still only six pence. In 1988 it was 30 pence, an increase of over twelvefold in 21 years! To avoid the toll you must make a detour of about two miles.

Eling has been a port for hundreds of years and ships were built here until the late 19th century. The quayside is chock-a-block with yachts now, but an occasional cargo-boat comes to load or unload. The size of the bollards is an indication of the size of the ships that once berthed here. The best view of the quay is from Goatee Park on the other side of the water. Henry I is said to have sailed to Normandy from Eling in 1130.

At a certain spot on the shore at Goatee Park you can see all seven crosses on the gables of St Mary's church, the only spot supposedly where this is possible. The footpath through Goatee Park takes you up into the churchyard, past the tomb-stone of two young men who were drowned while bathing at Testwood in 1872. The epitaph on the tomb of William Mans-bridge, who died in 1703, reads:

> Stop reader pray and read my fate
> Which caused my life to terminate
> For thievs by night when in my bed
> Broak up my hous and shot me dead

St Mary's church is indeed memorable for its tombstones and memorials, both inside and outside the building. Two of the memorials are by the famous sculptor Rysbrack.

Ellingham

➤ St Mary's church, hidden away at the end of a lane a short distance from the A338, has several unusual features. The large blue-and-gilt sundial above the porch is incongruous but fascinating. When checked by the Royal Observatory for accuracy in 1930 it was found to be only five or six minutes in error – an improvement on the mass-dial at least. Near the porch is the tomb of Dame Alice Lisle of nearby Moyles Court, who was executed in 1685 by order of the infamous Judge Jeffreys for sheltering supporters of the Monmouth rebellion.

The canopied family pew in the church is shaped like a medieval chantry chapel, probably because old chantry chapels had proved popular when used as pews. On the wall above the 15th-century screen are paintings of the Lord's Prayer, the Commandments, and the Creed. The reredos now at the west end of the church incorporates a 16th-century painting in the Mannerist style. John Wise said of it: 'whose bad execution is only exceeded by its indecent materialism'. No doubt he was rather shocked, but as a good Victorian churchman he should have known that not everybody wins on Judgement Day!

Ibsley, on the main road north of Ellingham, is an attractive little village with a thatched public house, The Old Beams Inn, and a bridge from which one can admire the distant views across the Avon valley. In the Georgian church (1832) there is a striking monument to Sir John Constable (died 1627) and his wife, which depicts the heads of their five children sprouting from a vine, an example of the inventiveness in design that was increasingly to characterize mid-17th-century monuments.

At Rockford, a mile east of Ellingham, there is a building unique in Hampshire – a public house that was once a village school. The Alice Lisle Inn is worth a visit for that reason alone – and it is a free house!

Emsworth

➤ Warblington was the original centre of the parish with the parish church. By the Middle Ages Emsworth had the larger population; it became the chief port of Chichester Harbour and the centre of a flourishing oyster-fishing industry. Its importance in Georgian times is reflected in the many houses of that period in the streets that radiate from St Peter's Square towards the quays and waterfronts.

King Street, formerly Sware Lane, was named after John King, a shipwright. His house, The Hut (No. 19 King Street), was built in 1795 in just a day, so the story goes. It is mainly of wood, the sections having been made in King's shipyard; the weatherboarding is flush and not overhung as is usual, and makes the house very attractive.

Queen Street, formerly Dolphin Hill, was renamed after the visit of Queen Victoria and Prince Albert in 1842. The Old Pharmacy in High Street has been a chemist's shop since 1812; it is said that the house at the back of it has a smugglers' room and an underground passage.

Sea bathing was already popular in England by the late 18th century. When Caroline, Princess of Wales, bathed in the sea while staying at Emsworth in 1805, the town had thoughts of becoming a royal watering-place like Bognor Regis. A bathing-house was built on the shore near the mill-pond, at the end of what is now Bath Road; it had baths supplied with fresh sea-water and heating facilities. The building is now the Emsworth Sailing Club. When the railway brought the working classes to Emsworth to bathe the gentry soon decided to go elsewhere.

P. G. Wodehouse lived between 1904 and 1913 (when not in London) at a house named Threepwood in Record Road, which is on the north side of Havant Road. He was a master for a few months at Emsworth House, a private school nearby (now destroyed), but what exactly he taught is not clear. Record Road is said to have been so named because of the record number of years in Queen Victoria's reign (63).

Eversley

Eversley is well-known for its association with Charles Kingsley, who was the rector here from 1844 to 1875. Visitors who come to see his grave and the old rectory where he wrote most of his books may not know of the house where he lodged before taking up residence in the rectory. Named Dial House because it has a splendid sundial on the wall, it stands just north of the road junction at Eversley Cross; it was known as The Brewery when Kingsley lived there.

A Charles Kingsley memorial overlooked by most visitors is at the Charles Kingsley School, at the junction of the A327 and Glaston Hill Road. The wrought-iron gates incorporate two figures of Tom, the boy in *The Water-Babies*, as a chimney-sweep and as a water-baby.

The village sign at Eversley Cross has the inscription '-EFORS LEIGH- FIELD of the WILD BOAR'. The name of the village was first recorded about 1050 as Evereslea, meaning 'boar's wood', from Old English *eofor* (boar) and *leah* (wood). *Efors Leigh* seems to be a mixture of old and new, *efors* (more commonly *eofors*) and *leigh* (a modern spelling).

One of the public houses at Eversley Cross is Le Toad and Stumps, which must surely be the most unusual public house name in Hampshire. Its former name was The Lamb, and before the village bypass was built there was a large pond in front of the inn. There is no hidden meaning to the name; it just sounded attractive to the new owner, though he was influenced by the many toads that lived nearby. The inn's bizarre name is in keeping with the rather strange interior decorations and signs, but not with the food, which is good.

John James, a leading architect of the early 18th century, is buried in St Mary's church. He lived at nearby Warbrook House and the church was rebuilt probably to his designs. He was one of the surveyors to the Commissioners appointed under the Church Building Act of 1711. His best-known churches are St Mary's, Twickenham and St George's, Hanover Square, London.

Gates of the Charles Kingsley School, Eversley

Exton

➤ Exton is an attractive little village on the west bank of the river Meon. Its public house, The Shoe, has a riverside garden. Beacon Hill, a National Nature Reserve north-west of the village, offers a superb view of the whole Meon valley; the Isle of Wight and much of the Hampshire coast is visible on a fine day.

A remarkable headstone in the parish church, commemorating Richard Pratt (died 1780) and his wife, depicts the Angel of Death summoning a scholar from his books. On the memorial to Dean Young of Winchester the date in his epitaph (1642) is hidden in a chronogram. It reads: 'VenI VenI MI IesV IVDeX VenI CIto'. Work it out! (see Nursling). He wrote his epitaph in troubled times, twelve years before he died.

The axis of the chancel is inclined at an angle to that of the nave. This peculiarity, fairly common in medieval churches, has often been suggested as symbolic of Christ on the Cross, the chancel representing His head leaning to one side. The truth is probably more mundane. Most medieval churches were built with little regard for mathematical accuracy, and few are in fact exactly rectangular. When churches were rebuilt these misalignments were usually but not always corrected.

Farley Chamberlayne

➤ The only place in this book not named on the Ordnance Survey 1:50,000 map, this remote hamlet in the parish of Hursley consists of a farm, a few houses and a church. Beyond it is Farley Down and the well-known Farley Mount.

The second half of its name is derived from the Chamberlain family who held the manor in the 12th century. In 1086 the manor had belonged to Herbert, son of Remigius, who was possibly the king's chamberlain; at some future date one of his descendants added his surname to the village name. There was almost certainly a medieval village here; the uneven ground between Farley Farm and the churchyard suggests a former settlement.

St John's church is Norman, except for the chancel; a pity the old box-pews and gallery were removed in 1910, for they would have enhanced its ancient homely atmosphere. Note the old timber roof with its tie-beams and king-posts. In the vestry is an iron cresset used for holding a beacon in times of emergency; it may have been used at the time of the Armada or even before then. From the churchyard you can see further than from almost any other Hampshire church.

One of the semaphore telegraph stations on the unfinished London to Plymouth line, a derelict one-storey building, stands in the field adjoining the church, but it is on private property and cannot be visited. The stations on either side were at Cheesefoot Head and Sherfield English (which also survives).

Farringdon

From 1797 to 1919 Farringdon had only two rectors. The second of these, Thomas Massey, who served for 62 years, was a most eccentric individual. His memorial stands opposite All Saints church, in the shape of the enormous red-brick building known as 'Massey's Folly', which must rank as one of the strangest buildings in Hampshire. It was designed and built by Massey himself, assisted only by a carpenter, a bricklayer and a labourer, and took 30 years to complete (1870–1900).

It is like no other building in Hampshire, or indeed in England. It has 17 bedrooms and two towers, and is profusely decorated with terracotta panels of the type popular in the late 19th century. It is uncertain what the building was intended for; it was used until recently as the village school, and part of it is still the village hall.

A certificate in the church from The Conservation Foundation, signed by the Archbishop of Canterbury and David Bellamy the biologist, states that one of the yew trees in the churchyard is over 3,000 years old. The yew has the longest life span of any British tree. *The Guinness Book of Records* states that the oldest yew in Great Britain, at Fortingall, Tayside, is about 3,500 years old.

Mary Winderbank was murdered in 1758 by a man who stole the money from under her bed. Her gravestone in the churchyard depicts a four-poster bed with money-bags under it, and a man dragging the old woman from it, urged on by the Devil. The inscription is mostly illegible but begins 'Murder most foul'.

Fawley

➤ At Ashlett there is an impressive four-storeyed brick-built tide-mill with a mansard roof, dated 1816. It was last used as a mill about 1890, and the mill-pond behind it is now used as a yacht basin. The popular Jolly Sailor inn has been here since at least 1870. Before the oil refinery was built Ashlett must have been a secluded little spot; even now at a quiet time of the day you get the feeling of being off the beaten track.

When the inhabitants of Tristan da Cunha had to evacuate their island in 1961 because of an erupting volcano they were eventually housed in the former Royal Air Force married quarters at Calshot. A model of one of their long-boats is in All Saints church; unfortunately the whereabouts of the church key seems to be a secret. In the churchyard is the grave of Flight Lieutenant Kinkead, who was killed in 1928 over the Solent while attempting to break the world air speed record.

Fordingbridge

➤ The medieval bridge and St Mary's church are well-known, but there are many other interesting and lesser-known buildings and objects hidden away in the old streets, such as the former workhouse, now the infirmary, and the mile-post marked 'Fordingbridge 0', south of the bridge.

In spite of its pretentious Town Hall (built as the Oddfellows Hall in 1877) Fordingbridge does not have a Town Council, even with a population of over 6,000. It is 'twinned' with Vimoutiers, a town in France near the famous 'cheese' village of Camembert.

A disastrous fire destroyed many houses in 1702; the total value of the properties lost was estimated then to be about

£5,000 (several £m in today's values). That is why so many houses are dated 1703 or soon after – it is an interesting exercise to see how many you can spot.

The most interesting place in Fordingbridge is the little-known museum at Sherings in Church Street. It is open only on Wednesday afternoons in summer, but is well-worth a visit, for it is a veritable treasure-house of memories. Sherings deserve much credit for amassing such an absorbing collection of rare and curious bygones from Fordingbridge and from further afield; it includes old woodworking tools, household appliances, motoring relics, toby jugs and mementoes of the First World War.

Augustus John, the famous artist, lived at Fryern Court, Upper Burgate, from 1928 to 1961. He is buried in the local cemetery and his statue stands in the recreation ground not far from the bridge. For his paintings, particularly his portraits, he was awarded the Order of Merit.

Bickton, a mile south of Fordingbridge on the bank of the river Avon, has the dubious distinction of being the village in Hampshire furthest from a railway station – it is twelve miles by road to Salisbury, the nearest one.

The former mill at Bickton stands on the site of a Domesday mill. Near the mill, between the two arms of the river, there is a 'floated' or 'floating' water-meadow, one of the many to be found in the chalkland river valleys, though few are now in use. A 'floated' water-meadow was flooded and drained by sluice-gates or weirs; the water carried lime and silt so inducing an earlier crop of grass, which meant that sheep could graze earlier in the year and thus save on stored food. The farmer could then afford more sheep, which in turn meant more manure for his arable fields, and so the irrigated water-meadow helped to increase agricultural production. It is thought that water-meadows were first worked in England in the 16th century. They were widely used until artificial fertilizers came into general use. A public footpath crosses this one.

Fritham

Fritham a small village in the parish of Bramshaw, lies almost in the heart of the New Forest; it consists of a farm, a few houses, a chapel and an old thatched public house, the Royal Oak. On weekdays at least it is a haven of peace.

A hundred years ago, however, it was not so quiet, for here was a gunpowder factory, owned by a German, Eduard Schultze, founded about 1863; John Wise (*The New Forest: its History and its Scenery*, 1863) mentions it as 'lately built'. The large pond at Eyeworth, fed by a chalybeate spring known as Irons Well, supplied water-power for the mills.

In its early days the factory made gunpowder for the Prussian army in the 1870 Franco-Prussian War; later it made smokeless sporting powder and finally closed about 1921. The factory covered an extensive area near the present Eyeworth Lodge. By 1900 about 70 men were employed on the day-shift and about the same number on the night-shift. They earned £1 a week and some of them walked six miles to work (by 7.0 am).

A school was built on forest land in Fritham in 1866; previously all the children had to walk to Bramshaw school. By about 1887 the older boys were again attending Bramshaw. Four pairs of cottages that were built for some of the workers still exist, and also a chapel built in 1904.

Schultze has even given a word to the *Oxford English Dictionary*, like Wellington and Cardigan. The entry under 'Schultze' reads: 'gunpowder, an explosive having nitrolignin as its chief constituent, first made in England in 1863'. There's fame for you!

In Studley Wood, about a mile north of Fritham, there is an earthwork known as Studley Castle (shown as 'Enclosure' on the Ordnance Survey map). This is the site of one of the royal hunting lodges that were built about 1360 in various places in the New Forest. They were timber-framed and roofed with Cornish or Purbeck slates, and had a surrounding ditch. Only a rectangular earthwork remains now as a reminder of the time when hunting was the chief leisure activity in the forest.

Funtley

➤ It is not generally known that the activities carried on at Funtley in the late 18th century changed the course of British history. Coalbrookdale in Shropshire is famous for the development of cast iron, but Funtley, equally important for the development of wrought iron, is little known.

The method of making wrought iron perfected here by Henry Cort almost certainly saved Great Britain from defeat by blockade in the Napoleonic Wars. Two-thirds of the wrought iron used in Great Britain until then had been imported from Sweden and Russia.

Cort used coal instead of charcoal as fuel, and finished iron bars by the use of grooved rolls instead of by a forge hammer; this increased the output in the average forge eight-fold. The term 'dry-puddling' was later given to Cort's revolutionary new process.

There had been a forge here in the 17th century, owned by the Earl of Southampton; Cort took over at Funtley in 1775. It is sad to relate that he died in poverty in 1800. The works was still operating in 1867 but was later destroyed by fire.

From the Titchfield–Wickham road a public footpath (along Ironmill Lane) passes the site; the lane is partly paved with ironstone and slag from the works. Though not much of the ironworks can be seen now, apart from a dam and a sluice, at least you are conscious of being at an historic place of the industrial past.

Grateley

➤ The Ordnance Survey names the village as Grateley and the parish as Grately, but the villagers probably don't lose any sleep over that peculiarity! A notice in the village proclaims: 'Here the first code of laws for All England was enacted by King Athelstan in 925 AD'. It depends on what is meant by 'here'; Athelstan almost certainly held a council in this vicinity at some date, perhaps at Quarley Iron Age hill-fort.

Though not perhaps 'the first code of laws', Athelstan's enactments formed the first legislation relative to lords and their servants, boroughs as trading centres, and a uniform coinage. Many of his laws dealt with the punishment of thieves, then as much of a problem as they are today.

A charity board in St Leonard's church states that Richard Pyle left '15/- yearly for the purchase of one great Coat', and also that William Earle, more generous or more wealthy perhaps, left 300 guineas the interest on which was to be spent on 'Beef and Cheese with Potatoes for the Poorest Families'. The 13th-century stained glass in one of the panels of the east window was saved and brought here in 1787 when most of the old glass in Salisbury Cathedral was destroyed by the architect James Wyatt.

Grayshott

➤ Flora Thompson (then Flora Timms), author of the trilogy *Lark Rise to Candleford*, came to Grayshott in 1897 at the age of 20 to work at the post office in Crossways Road. She was there for four years, staying at first with the postmaster and his family and later in lodgings. At that time Grayshott post office was used by many famous people, including George Bernard Shaw, who rented a house in the village, and Arthur Conan Doyle.

Soon after Flora left Grayshott to get married the postmaster, a man of violent temper, murdered his wife, but at his trial was declared insane. Another murder occurred in Crossways Road in 1915, when a Canadian officer savagely killed a sergeant; he too was declared insane. Flora Thompson returned to Hampshire in 1916 (see Bramshott). She wrote her famous books much later in life; she had to write in secret in her early days because her husband and his family sneered at her literary pretensions and her lowly upbringing.

The Fox and Pelican public house has a curious history. It was built in 1899 by the Grayshott and District Refreshment Association with the intention of encouraging the sale of non-alcoholic drinks. It sold alcohol also but that was kept out of sight. It was named the Fox and Pelican after Bishop Fox of

Winchester and the pelican in the crest of Corpus Christi College, Oxford, which the Bishop founded. It was opened by the wife of the Bishop of Winchester and so had ecclesiastical blessing; it even had a library of books donated by George Bernard Shaw.

The war memorial commemorates the dead of the Great War of 1914–*1919* (strictly correct because the Treaty of Versailles was signed in 1919) and of the Second War of 1939–1945 (usually referred to as the Second World War).

Greywell

Greywell is a very small parish and a good third of it is occupied by Butter Wood, an old mixed woodland on the London Clay. It is threaded by public footpaths but they have

Entrance to Greywell tunnel on the Basingstoke Canal

been diverted because of the M3 motorway, which effectively divides the wood into two halves. The village lies on a terrace above the river Whitewater, which rises less than a mile away.

The medieval St Mary's church stands in a delightful spot within a few yards of the river. Its outstanding features are the rood screen and its ceiling and the circular stair-turret that gave access to the rood. There is a footpath from the church to Greywell Mill upstream, but it is not recommended unless you are in jungle dress!

The entrance to Greywell tunnel on the Basingstoke Canal is near the road junction in the village. The tunnel is 1,230 yards long and was constructed in 1792; there is no tow-path and boats had to be 'legged' through by pushing the feet against the roof, while the horses went overland. The collapse of the tunnel roof in 1932 finally sealed the fate of the canal.

The Basingstoke Canal, from Weybridge to Basingstoke, was built as part of a scheme to link London with the English Channel and the Bristol Channel, but the connecting canals were never started. The canal thus served only the town of Basingstoke so it was never a financial success. From Greywell eastwards it is now an important freshwater wildlife habitat, and the tow-path is a good place for bird-watching and pike-fishing.

Hale

➤ The focal point of the village of Hale (from Old English *halh* meaning 'nook' or 'corner') is Hatchet Green, which was annexed by the Parish Council in 1975 because no owner could be traced. At the east end of the green is Windmill Ball, a circular mound where supposedly a windmill once stood, though the mound itself is almost certainly a Bronze Age barrow. A windmill is not shown on any of the old maps of this area.

At the west end of the green the cottage with thatched porches and dormer windows in its thatched roof was once a 'dame' school. A dame school was the 18th- and 19th-century equivalent of our primary school or nursery school. It was supervised by an elderly lady who charged each pupil a few pence per week, but the education received by the children was little or none. In the 18th century few children received any education worthy of the name; illiteracy was greater than in Tudor times and was increasing. A commission in 1861 reported that dame schools were both very common and very inefficient.

Thomas Shenstone in his poem 'The School-Mistress' (1742) gives a vivid picture of a dame school and its dame: 'A matron old, whom we Schoolmistress name;'. So does William Crabbe 70 years later in *The Borough*:

'That where a deaf, poor, patient widow sits
and awes some thirty infants as she knits –'

Charles Kingsley presents a more pleasant picture in *The Water-Babies* when Tom is given shelter by 'the nicest old woman that ever was seen' who looked after 'neat rosy chubby little children, learning their Chris-cross row.'

On the south side of the road from Hatchet Green to Hale Park (Hale Lane) is a perfect little classical lodge with a Doric portico. From the lodge a long avenue of trees runs down to Hale Park house. Beyond the house, on a wooded terrace above the river Avon, stands St Mary's church, which was rebuilt in 1717 by the architect Thomas Archer, who lived at Hale Park and is buried in the church. One of the leading architects of his time, his best-known buildings include St Philip's church, Birmingham (the Cathedral), St John's church, Smith Square, London, and Chatsworth House (the north front).

The part of Hale parish that lies within the New Forest is known as Hale Purlieu and belongs to the National Trust. It may once have been covered with pine trees but is now mainly heathland, except for Millersford Plantation, where the rare Dartford warbler has been seen.

Hamble

➤ There has been a ferry across the river Hamble to Warsash for several hundred years. John Leland used it in the 16th century on his way to Portsmouth. He described the Hamble estuary as a 'very fair rode for greate shippes' and Hamble village ('Hamelrise') as a good fisschar toun'. The ferry, a small motor boat, operates as and when required.

The priory of Hamble-le-Rice was established here in the early 12th century, and was later handed over to Winchester College. An inscription on some old stones near the War memorial states that they came from the priory situated on the south side of the church.

The narrow High Street sloping down to the river reminds one of a fishing village in Devon or Cornwall, until one notices the Hampshire bricks of the buildings. Rope Walk recalls the rope-making industry that flourished here, and Copperhill Terrace is named after the coppers in which the tar for preserving the ropes was boiled.

The Bugle inn claims that it dates from the 12th century ('when the Normans landed at Hamble-le-Rise'), and that its foundations were laid over 800 years ago. It was formerly named The Ferry House and parts of it are certainly very old.

In St Andrew's church there are memorials to many naval officers, including six admirals; one of them was Billy Douglas (died 1817), Admiral of the Blue Squadron. Before the last war Hamble became well-known for its aircraft factories and in Hamble Lane, on the site of the Folland factory, a Gnat aircraft built in 1960 is displayed (opposite The Harrier public house).

The memorial in the church to Sir Edwin Alliott Verdon-Roe (1877–1958), the famous pioneer aviator, states that he was the first Englishman to fly. This is not strictly true, at least without qualification. The first Englishman to fly was Henri Farman in 1907, though he lived and experimented in France. The first Englishman to make an officially recognised flight in England was J. T. C. Moore-Brabazon, over the weekend of 30th April–2nd May 1909. Verdon-Roe was the first Englishman to fly in England in an aircraft designed and constructed by an Englishman, on 13th July 1909. A previous flight by Verdon-Roe in

June 1908 was not 'officially observed' so was not recognised. The Wright brothers' flight in 1903 was not 'officially observed' either, but that has gone down in history as the first-ever flight.

One would not expect to find anything 'hidden' on Hamble Common and the shore but defence works of four periods of history can be seen there. The oldest, a prominent earthen bank and ditch running across the peninsula, may be the defences of an Iron Age fort. At the point where this bank meets the shore on the south side of the common there are scattered fragments of stone and masonry walling just below high-water mark. These are the remains of St Andrew's Castle, built about 1544 by Henry VIII as one of his coastal defence forts. A substantial building with three tiers of guns, it was destroyed in the Civil War. At the same spot, just above the beach, are the remains of a 19th-century gun battery, consisting of a gun platform and a large mound with a magazine. To complete the sequence there is a modern concrete gun emplacement near the car park.

Hambledon

➤ In the early 19th century the village of Hambledon was shabby and neglected; it had the familiar appearance of a once-prosperous village in decline. William Cobbett in his *Rural Rides* described it in 1826 thus: 'You see that it has been a considerable town. The church tells the same story; it is now a tumble-down rubbishy place;' (presumably referring to the village as 'tumble-down', but perhaps to the church as well).

Today it is quite different – clean, tidy and attractive, yet still retaining the atmosphere and appearance of a real old village, not one of the all-too-numerous 'beautified' places. A walk from the end of West Street to the far end of East Street reveals an astonishing variety of buildings. The house at Manor Farm is partly Norman; a terrace of old houses near it is named 'The Retreat' at one end and 'The Rest' at the other end. The building now Nos. 1–2 East Street was the village poorhouse in the 18th century.

This is a tale of two kings. The first is the fugitive Charles II (as he later became), desperately trying to evade capture after the Battle of Worcester in the Civil War. On Monday 13th October 1651 he arrived in Hambledon incognito and slept the night at the cottage on the Denmead road now named Kings Rest. The cottage and the larger house adjoining it (later called Bury Lodge) belonged to a yeoman farmer, Thomas Symons; the house was demolished in 1800 but not the cottage. The next day Charles made his way to Sussex and so to France. There was a price of £1,000 on his head, a large sum of money in those days.

The second king in our tale is George VI. On 22nd May 1944 Hambledon was chock-a-block with Allied troops and their vehicles preparing for the invasion of Europe. On that sunny summer day the King arrived to inspect them. The parade was held in Chestnut Meadow, opposite the very cottage where the future Charles II had stayed the night nearly 300 years before. One would like to think that King George was told of the royal connection of that historic place.

At the side of the road named Cams Hill, leading west out of the village, stands a large stone, a mute memorial to a savage murder that occurred one late evening in August 1782. On their way home after drinking at the New Inn were Nicholas Stares of Soberton and young John Taylor, a blacksmith from Hoe Cross. At this very spot Taylor suddenly attacked Stares, beating him to death with a mop handle and robbing him of a purse of money. He was later executed, and this stone was erected perhaps as a warning to others, because there was once an inscription on it that began 'Let future generations know'. It has always been known locally as the Murder Stone.

You must not leave Hambledon without visiting the parish church, for architecturally it is one of the most interesting in Hampshire. It could well serve as a textbook example of the various stages in the enlargement of a church from Saxon times to the 15th century. With the church guidebook you can follow the stages in its development; note particularly the remains of Saxon work in the nave walls.

Hartley Wintney

Unique among Hampshire villages, Hartley Wintney can best be described as a collection of greens and commons with houses around them and an old coaching road through the middle. Cricketers Green is the home of one of the oldest cricket clubs in the county, said to have been founded in 1770.

The road through the village was once the London to Exeter Coach road, and the settlement that grew up alongside the road was known as Hartley Row. The inns were always very busy – at least until the railway was built. The oldest of them is The Lamb Inn; the timber-framing of the side walls reveals its age.

The oak trees in orderly lines on The Common were planted after the Napoleonic Wars on the instructions of the lady of the manor, Lady Mildmay, as a future source of timber for building ships for the Navy. With the advent of iron ships the timber was fortunately not needed, so the trees remain to enhance the scenic beauty of the village. William Cobbett, on observing the plantation, wrote that 'they are planting oaks on the "wastes" as the "agriculturasses" call them' and praised her ladyship for preserving the soil. As well for his peace of mind that he did not know the real reason for planting the trees!

The medieval St Mary's church is some distance from the modern village, near the site of the medieval village. In the chuchyard are the graves of two generals as dissimilar in character as it is possible to imagine. One is General Hawley (nicknamed 'Hangman'), a soldier of the worst type who gained an unenviable reputation for severity to both the enemy and his own troops. He somehow contrived to lose the Battle of Falkirk to the Scots in 1745. In contrast Field Marshal Viscount Alanbrooke was a soldier to whom the country is forever in debt; but for his guidance and advice to Churchill in the Second World War the Allies might not have won.

At West Green House, the former home of General Hawley, there is a strange rusticated column with a Latin inscription that roughly translated means 'This monument was built with a great deal of money that otherwise some day would have been given into the hands of the public revenue'. There are several other follies in this delightful 18th-century garden, which is owned by the National Trust and is open to the public.

Hartley Wintney is 'twinned' with St-Savin in France, which is named after St Savinus the hermit and has a famous Norman abbey church.

Hatherden

➤ The oldest part of the village school is a charming two-storeyed brick building with a tiled roof; a plaque on it reads: 'This – Charity School for 24 Poor Children of Hatherden – Wild-Hern was endowed by James Sambourn Merchant Borne in Andover Obijt Oct:y- 20 1725 Dei Domum deo Datum'. Opened in 1727, it is one of the oldest schools still in use in Hampshire, but the building is even older. It was extended in 1873 and again in recent years, so it has parts built in three separate centuries; needless to say the most recent extension is the eyesore of the three.

Hatherden has two public houses, The Hamster (with a signboard picture of a well-dressed hamster in an armchair) and the Hare & Hounds, which stands at the five-way junction where the Roman road from Winchester to Cirencester passes. This Roman road was an important route from Winchester and the Channel ports to Cirencester, one of the largest Roman towns in the country. Most of the course of this road can be followed from Winchester to the Hampshire boundary on modern roads and tracks; through Hatherden and Tangley the agger is well preserved.

Hatherden is in the parish of Tangley. St Thomas's church at Tangley has a lead font, the only one in Hampshire. There are about 30 lead fonts surviving in England, mostly of the late 12th and early 13th centuries; this one is much later (early 17th century). Many lead fonts have been melted down over the years, often it is sad to relate by vicars and churchwardens.

Hawkley

➤ In November 1822 William Cobbett rode from Hawkley to Greatham and wondered whether he had ever seen worse roads. They are infinitely better now of course but still narrow, winding and often 20 ft or more below the top of the banks on either side.

In 1774 there was a huge landslip a mile east of the village. Though part of a prehistoric series of landslips flanking the Malmstone escarpment, it is the only recorded instance of renewed movement of one of these landslips in historical times. Natural landslips frequently occur on the coastal cliffs but this is possibly the only recorded case of such a slip in inland Hampshire.

Part of the escarpment subsided with deformation and fissuring of the ground below. A cottage was almost engulfed by the movements; this cottage, near Scotland Farm, was rebuilt and named Slip Cottage. The site of the landslip can be seen from the road above the cottage. The cause of the slip was the sliding of the Malmstone over the underlying Gault Clay after very heavy rain in the preceding months.

Gilbert White described the landslip in *The Natural History and Antiquities of Selborne*. He said that part of the hanger at Hawkley fell down perpendicularly in such a way that a gate fell 30 or 40 ft and yet still opened and closed perfectly. According to White the length of the slip was 251 yards, about 50 acres of land had 'suffered' and two houses were entirely destroyed. The *Hampshire Chronicle* reported that 60 acres of land had given way and a house was thrown down. Gilbert White's nephew said that nearly 1,000 people came to view the scene.

Hawkley Mill (1774), now a private house, stands beside a tributary of the river Rother. It has an inscription on the wall: 'Hocheleye Mill. Ancient mill of the Bishops of Winchester taken from them by Sir Adam Gurdon given back under King Edward AD 1280. Burnt down and rebuilt 1774. Became a cottage 1880. J.J.M.'

Adam de Gurdon, lord of the manor of Selborne and warden of Woolmer Forest, was a follower of Simon de Montfort and fought against Henry III. He lost a duel near Alton with Prince

Edward (later Edward I), who spared his life and restored his estates. The mill here is probably on the site of the one mentioned in Domesday Book as being at Empshott. In 1564 it was purchased by the warden of Winchester College.

Headley

 Of the many schools in Headley over the years only one survives. The Holme School was founded in 1755 by the rector of Headley and is still going strong, a few of its pupils being descendants of those who were taught there 234 years ago. At first it was known as Headley Charity School – twelve poor children were admitted free, the rest had to pay. Part of the present building appears to be original.

The agricultural labourers' riots of 1830 (see Amport) were particularly violent in Hampshire and marked by much destruction of property. At Headley the workhouse was attacked by a mob led by Robert Holdaway, a local wheelwright of normally excellent character. To what extent the house was damaged is not clear but it still stands, now Headley Grange, on the road to Liphook. 'Not a room was left entire' said the workhouse master at the subsequent trial.

Headley Mill on the river Wey is one of the few water-mills in Hampshire still producing flour. It has a 12½-foot-diameter water-wheel driving pairs of millstones. The stone-built mill makes an attractive picture with the waterfowl on the adjacent mill-pond. The ford over the river here is in the new parish of Lindford; the water-height indicator is pessimistically marked to a maximum of six feet.

The village war memorial records the names of 96 men killed in the First World War, and states that 619 also served. The population of Headley in 1914 (or 1911 to be precise) was 2,786 (3,836 including civilians at Bordon military camp). These figures illustrate the horrific impact of that war on villages such as this. In Great Britain 5,000,000 men served in the armed forces; nearly 2,000,000 of them were killed or wounded.

Herriard

A little-known museum at the north-east corner of Lasham airfield is owned by the Second World War Aircraft Preservation Society and is open to the public only on Sundays. In spite of its name most of the aircraft on display were built in the 1950s, and the Society deserves credit for rescuing them from destruction for the benefit of those interested in historic aircraft.

The aircraft on display include a Hawker Sea Hawk (the first jet design by Hawker), a De Havilland Vampire (the first jet fighter to operate from an aircraft-carrier), a De Havilland Drover, of which only 20 were built (mainly for the Royal Flying Doctor Service), a Hawker Hunter, two Westland helicopters, a Percival Sea Prince, one of the last Gloster Meteors to see service in the Royal Air Force, and a Starfighter designed by Lockheed and manufactured by Messerschmitt for the German Air Force.

Highclere

St Michael's church (1870 by George Gilbert Scott) is the result of an inflexible devotion to the Early English style of medieval architecture. In the 13th century narrow lancet windows made the interior of a church very dark; this did not matter because there were no Prayer Books and the congregation could not read anyway. The use of this style in 1870 however has resulted in a great deal of expense since then on artificial lighting. There are two interesting monuments, one to Sir Richard Kingsmill (died 1600) with figures of his kneeling children, the other to Thomas Milles, Bishop of Waterford, by Roubiliac.

A footpath from the village crosses Highclere Park to the cemetery that was first used in 1785. The designs for the park were made by 'Capability' Brown, the greatest of English landscape architects. He acquired his nickname from his habit of saying that a particular piece of countryside had 'great capabilities'.

Highclere had a station on the old Didcot, Newbury and Southampton Railway, but it was in Burghclere, over two miles away. The nearest station to Highclere village was Woodhay, which was in fact nearer to Highclere than to East Woodhay village. All very confusing!

A thrift club, said to be the first in Hampshire, was founded in Highclere. It met on Whit Mondays and held festivities at The Carnarvon Arms and afterwards at the Temple in the park. The girls dressed themselves in white and everybody ate large quantities of gingerbread. Its official name was the Hampshire and Dorset Deposit Society, but it was known locally as the Highclere Club or the Temple Club.

Hinton Ampner

Recorded in Domesday Book as Hentune, the manor belonged for centuries to St Swithun's Priory in Winchester and in particular to the almoner of the priory, hence the name of the present village – Hinton Ampner.

A church was mentioned in Domesday Book, and there are traces of that church in the present building, notably a Saxon doorway that now leads into the vestry. Many memorials to the Stewkeley family adorn the walls. Two prominent memorials were rescued from Laverstoke old church when it was demolished. One is an enormous tablet to Sir John Trott (died 1672) and the other a dramatic bust of Katherine Stewkeley (died 1679).

School House, on the main road, dates from 1730 and was a very early school, endowed under the will of William Blake, a groom who had married a daughter of one of the Stewkeleys. In use as a school until recently, much of it is original, including the square leaded windows.

Holmsley

The Old Station Tea Rooms was once Holmsley station on the Southampton and Dorchester Railway, which when opened in 1847 was one of the longest single-track lines ever

Milestone at Holmsley

constructed in England. A few years later the track was doubled. The line was known as 'Castleman's Corkscrew' because of the sinuous route that it followed, via Brockenhurst, Ringwood, Wimborne and Wareham. Castleman was the man behind the idea. Holmsley station was originally named Christchurch Road, being the nearest station to Christchurch, even though it was over seven miles away by the turnpike road. The main line via Sway and New Milton was not opened until 1888.

The platform where passengers waited for trains to Ringwood and Dorchester is still there. Those who could both read and afford a newspaper in 1847 would have seen that the first gold rush had started in California, that *Jane Eyre* and *Wuthering Heights* had just been published, that a new Factory Act limited the working day for women to ten hours, that an economic depression afflicted England, and that gorillas had been discovered in Africa.

At Spy Holms, north of Holmsley, large numbers of New Forest ponies can often be seen. The old road from Lymington to Ringwood skirts Spy Holms on the south; it has gone out of use within living memory. The half-way milestone (Lymington 7 Ringwood 7) stands not far from the main road.

Holybourne

◄ What must surely be the largest charity board in Hampshire is in the tower of Holy Rood church. It records at great length the details of the will of Thomas Andrews, who died in 1719. He left money for the building of a free school in Holybourne, at which children by the name of Andrews were to have preference. All the boys were to be taught writing and 20 of them Latin, and the girls were to be taught to work and read. The board, erected in 1784, was paid for by the 'voluntary subscriptions of the principle (sic) inhabitants of those parishes who are entitled to this benefaction'. Andrews Endowed School stands well back from London Road, an attractive early Georgian building of purple brick with red dressings.

Mrs Elizabeth Gaskell, the famous Victorian novelist, bought a house in the village in 1865 to give to her husband when he retired. She had to keep it a secret from him until the last moment because she knew that otherwise she could not have persuaded him to move from his beloved Manchester. She had therefore arranged to let it to a tenant until her husband's retirement. While staying at the house with her daughters in November of that year, prior to the tenant moving in, she collapsed and died. The house is The Lawn in London Road, almost opposite Church Lane.

Hordle

➤ The name Hordle may be derived from Old English *hord-hyll*, meaning 'treasure mound' or 'hill', but where exactly that may have been is anybody's guess. The name has had many forms over the years, starting with Herdel in Domesday Book, then Hordhull in 1242, Hordwell on the first Ordnance Survey map, and now Hordle.

By coincidence Hordle has two churches removed from their former locations though one, the old iron church at Tiptoe (opposite St Andrew's church), which came from Netley Hospital, is not used now as a church. All Saints, the parish church, which used to be nearer the coast (see Milford on Sea), was rebuilt two miles inland in 1830–1; because of its poor construction it had to be rebuilt again in 1872. The reason for its removal was not because of any danger of its falling over the cliff, as is sometimes supposed, but because it became dilapidated and most of the congregation lived a long way from it.

In the churchyard there is a massive granite memorial to John Collett (1798–1856). Its inscription reads: 'Rough as granite truth itself. Laborare est orare.' (To work is to pray.) Collett was a friend of poachers – he paid all their fines! Also buried in the churchyard, in unmarked graves, are Mrs Mary Girling and other members of a religious sect known as the 'Children of God' or more popularly as the 'Shakers' because of the manner in which they displayed their religious fervour.

They believed, among other things, in the common ownership of goods and that it was wrong to work for money (so they did no work!). They lived at Forest Lodge, now Hordle Grange, a nursing home (in Vaggs Lane); great crowds came to see them dancing or 'shaking'. One of Mrs Girling's beliefs was that she would live for ever, and when she died in 1886 her followers not surprisingly became rather disillusioned. At least two doctors had previously refused to certify her as insane, which perhaps says more about the doctors than about Mrs Girling.

Hordle is 'twinned' with Yerville, a village in France between Rouen and Dieppe.

Houghton

▬ At the north end of the village, on the road to Stockbridge, there is a strange little 'folly', an all-flint sham ruined castle that was built as a lodge to Houghton Lodge, the big house down by the river Test. Houghton Lodge was built about 1800, a house of the type known as cottage orné, a product of the cult of the picturesque favoured by the gentry of that time.

At the other end of this long straggling village on the west bank of the Test is Bossington Mill, three-storeyed and six-bayed, a plain but not unattractive brick building. At Horse-bridge the old station has been preserved more or less as it was when closed in 1964, complete with waiting-room, parcel office, signal box, signals, platforms, and an L&SWR third-class coach, almost everything in fact except the track, and a nostalgic scene it really is. The Test Way footpath runs along-side the station.

All Saints church has one unusual feature – asymmetrical nave arcades, two bays on the north, three bays on the south. There were five rectors in the year 1348, the year of the Black Death; three of them died of the plague.

Hursley

➤ Richard Cromwell was living at Hursley when his father Oliver died in 1658. He was summoned to London to take over as Lord Protector of England, but two years later was deposed and fled to the Continent. He never saw his wife again. After an absence of 20 years he returned to England and lived to the age of 86. He was buried under the chancel of All Saints church but the exact whereabouts of his grave is not known because the church has been rebuilt twice since then. There is a memorial in the tower to members of the Cromwell family.

The present church was paid for by the rector, John Keble, who with his wife is buried in the churchyard. Its style (neo-Decorated) was dictated by the Victorian Ecclesiology movement; the interior, formal, lifeless and meticulously medieval, exemplifies the Gothic Revival of the mid-19th century. The tower, the one true medieval feature, once had a spire.

The timber-framed cottages on the main road (Nos. 97A, 97 and 98A) have lattice windows and are probably 16th century. Their upper storeys overhang in typical medieval fashion, supported on beam-ends and brackets. No. 97 has a hanging shutter that was used as a counter when the house was a shop.

House No. 42 has three tall 18th-century chimneys, each of a different shape. Not many small houses had chimneys before the time of Elizabeth I but when it was found that brick was very heat-resistant chimneys gradually became universal. For structural reasons they were usually in the centre of the house, and visually that is undoubtedly the best place for them.

The Hursley Union workhouse covered at first only four parishes (Hursley, North Baddesley, Otterbourne and Farley Chamberlayne) and was the smallest Union in England; later it incorporated two more (Ampfield and Chandler's Ford). The Union was moved to Chandler's Ford in 1900. The workhouse was in a building adapted from a row of cottages; its two long blocks at right angles to the road have been converted back again to houses (The Square in Collins Lane).

Some medieval deer park banks, or pales as they are called, have an almost military appearance and the one at Hursley is a good example. Part of it can be seen alongside the Romsey to Winchester road south of the village. Further long stretches run through Ampfield Wood (the footpath from Knapp to Hursley crosses them). Note the wide ditch on the inside of the park pale; it was once deep enough to discourage the deer from leaping over the bank and escaping.

The deer park was owned by the Bishop of Winchester, who had parks at nine of his ten Hampshire residences. (The King had six parks in Hampshire.) The labour involved in making this huge bank and ditch, four miles long, must have been colossal, but bishops of the Middle Ages were powerful men who could summon as much forced labour as they needed.

Hurstbourne Priors

➤ The village lies on a terrace on the west side of the Bourne rivulet, which here joins the river Test. St Andrew's church stands between the village and the river, at the end of an avenue of beech trees.

The most interesting memorial in the church is the tomb of Sir Robert Oxenbridge (1574), which in addition to the effigies of himself and his wife has kneeling figures of their twelve children, six of whom are holding skulls to show that they died during their parents' lifetime.

From 1380 to 1520 nearly all the rectors were knights, and were probably absentee rectors who employed a curate to look after the church services for them (see St Mary Bourne).

Thatch seems to have been popular here, not only for houses such as Longthatch (near The Hurstbourne public house) but also for the cricket pavilion and the bus shelter.

One of the regulations for the use of the recreation ground reads: 'No person shall fly any jet-propelled or rocket-propelled aircraft in the ground.' With natural hazards such as tall trees it is unlikely that anybody would try!

At the May Day festivities in days gone by one of the highlights was the 'Jack in the Green' ceremony, in which chimney-sweeps rattling their shovels and brushes danced round a man disguised as a tree. The origin of this curious activity is not known, but they must have looked and sounded rather like certain modern 'pop' groups.

Hurstbourne Tarrant

➤ Of all the places that William Cobbett visited regularly Hurstbourne Tarrant was his favourite. He commented on its more popular name in his *Rural Rides*: 'This place is commonly called Uphusband, as decent a corruption of names as one would wish to meet with. However, Uphusband the people will have it . . .'. In 1826 he described the village thus: 'The houses of the village are, in great part, scattered about, and are amongst very lofty and fine trees; . . . the village is a sight worth going many miles to see. The lands, too, are pretty beyond description.' But his enthusiasm for the village was tempered by his sadness at the living conditions of the people. He wrote: 'For, I have, in no part of England, seen the labouring people so badly off as they are here.'

He stayed in the village with his friend James Blount of Rookery Farm (now Rookery House), which he called his 'free quarters'. A solidly-built Georgian farmhouse on the main road at the foot of Hurstbourne Hill, it is surrounded by Cobbett's 'very lofty and fine trees'; they are full of rooks, as they probably were in those days too and hence gave the farm its name. James Blount's grave is in the churchyard, his tombstone very large and flat so that the village children could play marbles on it, it is said!

The stream (now often dry) that flows through the village is the river Swift. Its source is at Upton and at Hurstbourne Tarrant it meets the Bourne rivulet, which rises near Lower Farm. The George & Dragon is the only remaining inn of the many that once served the village people and travellers on the highway.

St Peter's church has a rare wall-painting of the legend of the three living kings and the three dead kings. According to this legend, attributed to the 13th-century French writer Baudouin de Condé, three kings out hunting met three skeletons, which reminded them that their days too were numbered. The 17-foot-long thatch-hook under the tower was used in the days before fire brigades to pull down burning thatch from houses, or the houses themselves if necessary.

Hythe

➤ Hythe pier, the longest on the south coast (2,100 ft), is not exactly a hidden object, but some facts relating to it are not so well-known. It was opened to the public on 1st January 1881 and is one of only three or four in England with their own railway. The track was electrified in 1922 and uses two Brush locomotives, bought from the Avonmouth mustard gas factory, which have run continuously for 67 years at double their original intended voltage.

The Drummond Arms (family arms 'Lord have mercy') facing the pier and The Lord Nelson in High Street with its 'quaint bars' are still in business, but sadly the Anchor and Hope on the corner of High Street is no longer an inn – the derivation of its name conjures up weird possibilities.

T. E. Lawrence (Lawrence of Arabia) spent some time at Hythe in 1931–32 while serving in the Royal Air Force under the name of T. E. Shaw. He was employed on the testing of high-speed air-sea rescue launches and wrote a manual entitled *Notes on Handling the 200 Class Seaplane Tender*, which must be rarer than most of his other books. While at Hythe he lodged during the week at Myrtle Cottage, which stands at the junction of South Street and Shore Road. At weekends he returned to his Dorset cottage.

Itchen Abbas

➤ Itchen Abbas can justifiably claim to be in the heart of Hampshire, because half a mile north-north-west of the village is the point furthest from any part of the county boundary (about 16 miles). It is only a short distance from the site of a Roman villa that was excavated in 1878, where mosaics, coins and pottery were found.

In the churchyard is the grave of John Hughes, a gypsy hanged in 1825 at the age of 26 for horse-stealing. He is said to have been the last man in England to be hanged for this offence. Though at that time theft still carried the death penalty it was seldom meted out; the judge in this case decided to make an example of Hughes to deter others.

Between the years 1800 and 1901 the parish church had only three rectors. The first of these was Robert Wright, rector for 50 years. He was at home at all levels of society, being not only a great friend of the poor but also chaplain to the Duke of Wellington. He was responsible for seeing that gypsy John Hughes had a decent burial. The church was rebuilt in 1862–3, unusually for that date in the Norman style, and incorporated the chancel arch from the old Norman church.

The ugly pebble-dashed village hall was partly paid for by Sir Edward, later Viscount Grey, the longest-ever-serving British Foreign Secretary, who often came to stay at his fishing cottage here in the early years of this century. It was Grey who said in 1914: 'The lamps are going out all over Europe'. Charles Kingsley also enjoyed fishing in the river Itchen, famous for its trout, and it is said that he wrote *The Water Babies* while staying at Itchen Abbas.

Itchen Stoke

➤ Itchen Stoke and Ovington is one of the longest parishes in the county but is very narrow, at its widest only a mile and a quarter. It extends over eight miles from Abbotstone Down and its prehistoric camp (inappropriately named Oliver's Battery) to the village and the river Itchen and up the other side of the valley to Longwood Warren. But it has no shop, no post office and only one public house (but a very popular one), The Bush Inn at Ovington.

Abbotstone in the north of the parish was recorded in Domesday Book as having a mill and land for five ploughs. It was a flourishing community right up to the Black Death, which hit Hampshire particularly hard. In the fields on the east side of the stream are the terraced sites of the medieval houses; in 1327 there were at least 18 homes and a church. The whole site is now designated an Ancient Monument. The five ancient roads and tracks that meet on the west side of the stream suggest that in those days Abbotstone stood at an important junction of ways.

St Mary's church at Itchen Stoke, designed by the vicar's architect brother in 1866, is impressive with its rich decoration and long high nave, but its design, based on the church of Sainte-Chapelle in Paris, seems oddly out of place here. It is not used now, being in the care of the Redundant Churches Fund. There are two old brasses in the church, one of about 1500 of an unknown kneeling lady and the other dated 1518 of Joan Batmanson.

An interesting curiosity is in the floor of the apse, the tiles of which are set in the form of a maze similar to the one in Chartres Cathedral, the largest still surviving of the many that once existed in French cathedrals (see Breamore). Most have been destroyed for various reasons, the one at Reims because children made too much noise tracing its path during services.

The Old School, built in 1830, is opposite the church. In the 1870s non-attendance by the pupils was a problem. Bad winter weather and infectious diseases were partly to blame, but the horse-races on Abbotstone Down were also a bad influence. On one race-day in 1876 only eight children were at school!

Kingsclere

➤ Kingsclere is an ancient place with a long history; it was once a royal manor owned by King Alfred. At the time of Domesday Book (in which it is named simply Clere) it received income from a toll, one of the only two in Hampshire (the other one was at Titchfield). Its situation, at the foot of the Hampshire downs at the junction of roads from Newbury, Whitchurch, Basingstoke and Reading, added to its importance. It was once the second-largest parish in Hampshire.

Today Kingsclere is a place where many buildings have changed their use. In Pope's Hill and Tower Hill, The Old Malthouse, The Granary, The Maltings, The Old Brewery

House and Brewery Cottage are private houses now but were once part of the brewing industry in this area. Falcons, near the church, and No. 46 Swan Street were once inns; the former was owned by the Archbishop of Canterbury and used as lodgings by royal messengers.

There were four mills on the little stream that flows through the village; three of them still exist but are mills no longer. Gaily Mill, once known as Kingsclere Mill, is near the source of the stream. The Old Mill in Pope's Hill (very smart in its white paint) was formerly Town Mill, and Island Mill further downstream was formerly known as Lower Mill. Finally in our catalogue of changes the grim red-brick Albert Hall of 1886 in Swan Street is now a Catholic church. Why was it called the Albert Hall? Its London namesake was completed in 1870.

In spite of all these changes, and some new buildings, much of the ancient townscape remains, especially in Swan Street where The Swan Hotel and No. 24, both early 18th century, stand out. George Street is not so attractive, but No. 8 with its walls of rammed chalk and flint is possibly 16th century. North Street with its large 18th-century and 19th-century houses is quiet and pleasant.

The interior of St Mary's church is very bare, for the only monument or memorial to be seen (other than those in the chapel, which is not open) is the one to Sir Richard Kingsmill. It is a splendid piece erected by his widow in 1670, 45 years after his death at the age of 38. This type of tomb, with recumbent effigies, was becoming uncommon at this time and was out of fashion completely by 1700, but was revived in the 19th century.

The weather-vane, shaped rather like a bed-bug, is the subject of a well-known but probably apocryphal story. It is said that King John spent a restless night at the local inn because of these creatures, and ordered the church to display one on its tower for evermore. Its rather vague shape has also been likened to a winged dragon or a tortoise, so you must take your pick!

Kingsclere has been famous for its horse-racing stables for a long time; the downs above the village provide the perfect training-ground. The local stables produced seven Derby winners in the 19th century.

From White Hill on the summit of the downs (a splendid view over the Berkshire vale) take the Wayfarer's Walk to Watership Down, made famous by Richard Adams in his novel. Many places on and below the downs feature in the book. One of them is Nuthanger Farm, across the road at the foot of the downs, where Hazel and Fiver were chased by a cat.

Some old place-names and field names in and around Kings-clere are interesting and amusing. Spirits Mead, Nothing Hill, The Seven Phlixes, Great Clinkers, Long Cuts, Galldrops, Nickleydew's Copse, Scrotches, and Fosberry's Piddle leave a bit to the imagination!

King's Somborne

➤ There is a tradition that John of Gaunt, the English prince and fourth son of Edward III, had a palace at King's Somborne, situated perhaps in the field south of the church. There is little or no evidence to substantiate the story; excavations near the site in 1984–5 produced evidence of an Anglo-Saxon settlement but nothing more. There was a house there in 1591, owned by the Crown, described as 'a verey fayer and Anncyent House' with mills, orchards, gardens and walls.

John of Gaunt has also given his name to the deer park that was situated between the village and the river Test. The boundary bank or pale can be traced nearly all the way round the park and is the best preserved of those surviving in Hampshire; alongside the Horsebridge road it is seen at its best, up to twelve feet high.

When the Reverend Richard Dawes became vicar in 1836 he found the inhabitants of King's Somborne to be of rather low character and demoralised by the old Poor Law regulations. He decided that education of the children was the answer; at that time they received very little, and the farmers who employed many older children were against it. With a grant from the National Society for Promoting the Education of the Poor in the Principles of the Established Church, Dawes in 1842 founded the school that adjoins the church. It soon became probably the best-known village school in England for the quality of its teaching, and was often cited as a model school. Even the Prime Minister paid a visit to see it for himself. Central to the teaching was an emphasis on the reading and writing of English as the key to all the other subjects; a pity that principle is no longer upheld in English education.

The war memorial was designed by Edwin Lutyens, the famous architect of the Cenotaph in London. He also designed Marsh Court, the large house of great originality overlooking the Test valley near Stockbridge, built most unusually of chalk ashlar.

Another memorial, much simpler and hidden away, lies at the side of the public footpath that follows the Roman road east of Hoplands. A stone is inscribed: 'To 4 unknown German airmen. Aug 23 1940.' A sobering thought that even at the height of a war one's enemies can be so remembered, at a spot over which other enemies marched some 1,900 years ago.

The smallest church in Hampshire is situated at remote Upper Eldon on the road to Braishfield. A single-celled late-Norman building measuring 32 ft by 16 ft, it has not been used for services since 1971 and is in the care of the Redundant Churches Fund.

The Test Way footpath follows the course of the disused Andover and Redbridge Railway and a mile north of Horsebridge station crosses the Clarendon Way footpath, which here crosses the Test valley from Houghton to King's Somborne. The John of Gaunt tradition has lost none of its appeal, because the Railway Inn at Horsebridge has been renamed the John of Gaunt.

Kings Worthy

➤ The Old Post Office near St Mary's church claims to be the earliest post office not only in Hampshire but also in England. The earliest type of post office was known as a receiving house, where letters were handed in and collected; after the introduction of postage stamps the post offices became more like those of today. A receiving house was opened in Kings Worthy in March 1845, and a Post Office Archives list names it as one of the six earliest in the country. The Old Post Office was the post office from 1866 to 1966, but whether it was the one that opened in 1845 is not known. A letter-box in Winchester Museum is described as coming from 'Kings Worthy – the oldest post office in the country'.

The inscription on the headstone in memory of James Parker in St Mary's churchyard may give a clue to the way he died (on 8th April 1886) – 'The enemy hath smitten my life down to the ground'. Parker, an 18-year-old seaman, had arrived in South-ampton the previous week. With another member of the ship's crew, Albert Brown, he had set out to walk to London; they called at the Hyde Tavern in Winchester on the way. The next morning Parker's mutilated body was found in a field at the foot of Barton Hill. Meanwhile Brown had taken a train to London, where he was arrested and charged with murder. After being sentenced to death Brown confessed to the crime and told the police where the murder weapons (a hammer and a razor) could be found. The money for the headstone was subscribed by residents of Kings Worthy.

Laverstoke

In 1712 Henry Portal, a young Huguenot refugee from France, commenced paper-making at Bere Mill on the river Test. He was so successful that in 1719 he moved to the newly-completed Laverstoke Mill, and in 1724 obtained the contract to make the paper for Bank of England notes. The firm of Portals still makes it (at Overton) 265 years later.

The picturesque weatherboarded Bere Mill still stands by the Test, a charming scene from the bridge upstream. Laverstoke Mill has been rebuilt; the present building dates from the mid-19th century and paper-making ceased there in 1963.

A plaque on No. 6 Laverstoke Lane reads: 'The "Little White Tenement next the Mill" built by Joseph Portal as a Residence for the Bank Officer 1785'. Mr Still, the Bank Officer, claimed as part of his yearly expenses: Rent of the house £2.12s.6d., a chaldron of coal £1.17s.0d., and three bottles of old port 4s.6d. Further along Laverstoke Lane are the flint-and-brick cottages

Bere Mill by the river Test at Laverstoke

built for the mill-workers, standing on each side of the incongruous modern Sports and Social Club annexe.

At Freefolk, on the road to Whitchurch, a long row of almshouses catches the eye; known as Manor Cottages, they are of brick with half-timbered gables, the roofs half thatch and half tiles. They were built by Portals in 1939, but their vernacular Arts and Crafts style could easily be mistaken for something 30 years older. Across the road from them is a tiny public garden with a seat made from an old fountain.

Hidden away down the lane opposite Manor Cottages, across the river Test (a beautiful stretch just here), is the little rustic church of St Nicholas. It is difficult to date it precisely; it was restored in 1703 and its interior character reflects that date. This church is probably the successor to the one mentioned in Domesday Book. The imposing tomb of Sir Richard Powlett of Herriard (died 1614) shows him reclining on his side with his two kneeling wives.

Lee-on-the-Solent

Three things that Lee-on-the-Solent no longer possesses – its railway, pier and tower – are more interesting than anything still visible. Passenger trains were abandoned in 1930, but the demolition of the pier in 1958 and the tower in 1969 finally proved that Lee-on-the-Solent had not made the grade as a major seaside resort. Development was started in 1884 by Sir J. C. Robinson, after his son had seen the site from his yacht and recommended it to his father.

The 750-foot-long pier was opened in 1888, and in 1935 a 120-foot-high tower was built at its landward end; the only evidence of the pier now is the name Pier Street, opposite the site of the pier. It lasted longer than the railway, which was opened in 1894 and finally closed to goods traffic in 1935. The railway was built in the hope that Lee-on-the-Solent would become another Bournemouth, but it was never able to compete successfully with the Gosport bus service. There is no trace of its track but it ran between the beach and the promenade, starting from Fort Brockhurst on the Fareham to Gosport line.

The station building (now Olympia Amusements) survives but nothing else.

The Fleet Air Arm Memorial on the front lists all the members of the Fleet Air Arm who died in the Second World War – about 1,800 names.

There are at least two old buildings in Lee-on-the-Solent, both in Manor Way. Le Breton Farm, built in 1370 according to the *Hampshire Treasures Survey*, is a strange survival among the Edwardian villas and post-war houses. Near it the Bun Penny public house, formerly the Victoria Hotel, is said to be an 18th-century coaching inn.

Lepe

It is said that there was once a causeway from Lepe to the Isle of Wight and that at one place people had to leap over a gap, hence the name. There is no evidence for the causeway but the name may indeed be derived from Old English *hliep*, meaning 'leaping place' (ie over the stream named Dark Water). The name was first recorded in 1277. John Wise had a different explanation; he said that it was derived from Old English *leap*, meaning 'a basket for catching fish'.

Lepe was once a more important place than it is now. Three warships were built here in the 18th century, and some of the Mulberry harbours were assembled here in the Second World War. The odd-looking building on the shore, below the 19th-century slate-hung coastguard cottages, is The Watch House, which as its name implies was once the coastguard station, ideally placed to observe boats entering the Beaulieu river.

A public footpath, the only one on the entire stretch of coast between Calshot and Lymington, follows the shore for about a mile westwards as far as an old quay, near which there were once two brickworks, as recalled by the nearby Brickyard Cottages. This is as peaceful a walk as you will find on the Hampshire coast; very likely your only companions will be multitudes of sea-birds, but the path may be impassable at high tide.

Liss

West Liss is the original village, with picturesque St Peter's church and its 13th-century tower. The church porch, of which the base at least is original, is dated 1639 with an inscription 'Henry Haines Gift' and quotations from two psalms. Church Street has a neat row of old cottages, and on the main road the almshouses of 1881 were built 'chiefly for the widows of agricultural labourers of Liss.'

East Liss grew with the coming of the railway in 1859. The names of two of its public houses, The Crossing Gate (formerly the Station Hotel) and The Whistle Stop (formerly the Railway Hotel), acknowledge the part played by the railway in the development of the village. By 1871 the parish had a population of almost 1,000.

The Flying Bull public house on the A3 at Rake is partly in Hampshire and partly in West Sussex. The county boundary runs through the Two Counties Bar; a notice hanging from the ceiling indicates the exact line. It is said that before the inn was rebuilt the kitchen oven was exactly on the boundary and in 'beating the bounds' of the parish a small boy had to be pushed into it. The Flying Bull is not unique in Hampshire. The Red Lion at West Dean is partly in Hampshire (in West Tytherley parish) and partly in Wiltshire and there too the drinks are served in Hampshire; at the time of writing however the Red Lion is under threat of closure.

The previous inn here at Rake was the scene of a furious gun-fight one day in 1786. After the murder of an unknown sailor at Hindhead the murderers were apprehended and captured at the inn after trying to shoot their way out. The name Flying Bull is said to be derived from two famous coaches that used this road, the 'Fly' and the 'Bull', but Larwood and Hotten (*English Inn Signs*) state that it was coined by a facetious innkeeper as a reply to the inns with the name Flying Horse.

Littleton

➤ You might pass Littleton church without a second glance, assuming it to be of no interest, but it is worth a visit. It is dedicated to St Catherine the Martyr of Alexandria (of Catherine wheel fame), a popular saint in the Middle Ages, and was rebuilt in 1884–5. The Purbeck marble font is Norman and a fine example of its type. Two old brasses on a gravestone commemorate John Smyth (died 1505) and his wife Alicia (died 1493). The strangest tombstone is that of 'Temperrences, wife of Richard Fiffild of Head Borinwoorthy' (Headbourne Worthy). One wonders what she was called for short! In the churchyard at Crawley is the grave of the daughter of Mrs Temperance Vince, so the name was not that unusual, at least in this locality.

Outside the church is the grave of William Butler, who died at the age of 74; for 55 years he was the servant of a Mr Dilly. One hopes that Mr Dilly deserved such faithful service; which of them died first is not stated. The church has a 'weeping chancel' (see Exton).

Near the church is Monks Rest, a 17th-century house with a brick-and-flint chimney-piece. It was formerly the priest's house and later was the village school.

In the recreation ground are two Bronze Age barrows. One of them is a disc barrow, one of the largest of this type in England, nearly 200 ft in diameter. There is also an enormous sarsen found in 1906. Sarsens are boulders of hard sandstone found in the chalklands of southern England. They were often used in the construction of prehistoric burial places and stone circles, and are also known as grey wethers, from their supposed resemblance to grazing sheep. The name sarsen is a corruption of Saracen, ie something foreign.

Longparish

➤ The name Longparish, which has superseded Middleton as the name of the village, is an apt one because the village stretches for three miles along the Test valley. Its railway station, on the Hurstbourne–Fullerton line, was on the other side of the A303 a long way from the centre of the village. It is now a private house (Smallwood Lodge), its date prominently marked (AD 1884). Here in 1927 *The Ghost Train* was filmed, the first of the three films of that name (see Burghclere). Opposite the old station the Test Way follows a track down to Gavelacre, a secluded hamlet on the bank of the Test.

In that part of the village still known as Middleton there are several roadside curiosities. At the corner by the church of St Nicholas is an imitation Saxon cross dated 1867 and inscribed 'Via Crucis Via Lucis', and near the lich-gate is a set of stocks, a reproduction of the original, dating from about 1930. A half-mile north-east of the church, beyond Sugar Lane, stands a grinding wheel on a wooden pedestal, in perfect working order, and a few yards further is an old well with two oak seats and carved surrounds, presented in 1868 and known as Ash Burn Rest.

Road accidents are not entirely a new phenomenon, as a gravestone in the churchyard testifies. Robert Burns, a bombardier in the Army, lost his life 'near this place by an Accident from a Road Waggon' on 26th September 1796.

Longparish has two recent claims to fame. In 1986 it was adjudged Hampshire's best-kept village in the annual competition for that title ('impossible to fault it' said the judge), and in 1987 its cricket team beat Treeton Welfare by 76 runs in the final of the National Village Knock-out Trophy at Lord's.

Now to the most hidden curiosity in the whole of Hampshire. In Harewood Forest, between the A303 and the Middleton–Andover Down road, there is a monument, a large one but difficult to find in the summer when the foliage is thick. It is almost impossible to describe its position – look on the Ordnance Survey map, where it is marked with a dot and the word 'Monument'. It was erected in 1825 by Lt-Col William Iremonger and is known as Deadman's Plack, an apt name as the story inscribed on it reveals:

About the Year of our Lord DCCCCLXIII Upon this Spot beyond Time of Memory. Called Deadman's Plack   Tradition reports that Edgar (Surnamed the Peaceable) King of England in the ardor of Youth Love and Indignation Slew with his own hand his treacherous and ungrateful Favourite Earl Athelwold owner of this Forest of Harewood in resentment of the Earl's having basely betrayed his Royal confidence and perfidiously married his Intended Bride The beauteous Elfrida Daughter of Ordgar Earl of Devonshire afterwards Wife to King Edgar and by him Mother of King Etheldred the IInd, which Queen Elfrida after Edgar's Death murdered his eldest Son King Edward the Martyr and founded The Nunnery of Wher-well.

Iremonger must have believed this story to have gone to all the trouble of erecting a monument in this lonely spot. The historians Macaulay and Freeman however both thought it no more than a legend, embroidered by William of Malmesbury in the 12th century from an old ballad. The death of Athelwold at about that time and Edgar's marriage to Elfrida are true enough but nothing more is known for certain.

Longstock

◄ The name of The Peat Spade Inn recalls the days when peat was dug from the valley for fuel. The river Test flows past the village but you cannot walk alongside it – between Southampton and Whitchurch there is no public footpath anywhere along its banks.

In a piece of woodland near the inn are the supposed remains of a Danish dock or harbour, forming three sides of a square. Only two or three of these Danish sites have been recognised in England, and if this is also one it must obviously predate the bridge at Stockbridge for boats to have reached it. The site is on private land and may not be visited.

A few yards south of the A30 on the road to Houghton is

Drovers House, which was once an inn or guest-house used by Welsh drovers. The inscription in Welsh on the front means: 'Seasoned hay, tasty pastures, good beer, comfortable beds'. (The first two for the animals presumably.) Adjoining it is Cossacks, formerly the Cossack public house, named after the Derby winner of 1847 who was trained at the nearby Danebury stables.

Further along the road is Hermit Lodge, where the Prince of Wales (the future Edward VII) often stayed when attending the races at Stockbridge. His mistress, Lily Langtry, would stay at The White House across the river and visit him via the footbridge. Hermit Lodge was named after the Derby winner of 1867, who was buried in the garden opposite. Hermit won by a neck at odds of 1,000–15 after ten false starts; heavy snow fell (on 22nd May!) before and after the race.

Lymington

Lymington became a borough sometime between 1184 and 1216, one of the earliest in England. Its most important industry and trade in the Middle Ages was salt, but smuggling must have been a close second.

The salt exchequer office is said to have been at The Chequers inn at Woodside, and that that was how the inn got its name. But 'chequer' is a word that once meant any place where money transactions were carried on. There is no proof that the inn was the local salt office, but it does have strange cast-iron window-frames, perhaps for security at that time.

Two old brick buildings beyond The Chequers were connected with the salt industry. They stand at the head of a creek known as Moses Dock, where barges brought in coal and took out salt. The Solent Way footpath follows the coast from here to Keyhaven. These marshes form a nature reserve of great interest and the variety and number of native and visiting birds are unequalled in Hampshire. You are advised to keep to the public footpath.

At several places on the Solent Way between Moses Dock and Lymington remains can be seen of the old salt-pans, square enclosures with low mud walls where sea-water was allowed to evaporate and the salt extracted.

Daniel Defoe wrote that smuggling was the 'reigning commerce of the whole south coast'. Everywhere under the town there are said to be tunnels that were used by smugglers to get their booty from the quay to inns and houses. Another uncivilised activity, but one encouraged by authority, was carried on by the press-gangs, who forcibly conscripted men into the Navy. They were supposed to recruit only paupers, vagabonds and criminals, but many luckless victims were caught by them. Pressgang Cottage in Bath Road has a sign stating that it was once the Harlequin inn, headquarters of the press-gangs in about 1800.

Lymington has a higher percentage of retired people than any other town in Hampshire (about 30%). It also has an inordinate number of public houses, but there is no connection between the two because most of the public houses have been there longer than the retired people have. There were once 45 inns in Lymington!

Some of those still to be seen include The Fighting Cocks, The Famous Black Cat (famous?), the Borough Arms (formerly the Clipper), The Angel Inn (with wrought-iron balcony), and the Tollhouse Inn. Those that are inns no longer include the Alarm (c.1680) and the Solent in Quay Hill, and the Dolphin (c.1680) in Quay Street.

What must surely be the best-preserved and most picturesque toll-house in Hampshire adjoins the Tollhouse Inn in Southampton Road, which was formerly the Lymington to Southampton turnpike road (enacted 1765). The toll-house was probably built many years later.

A stone set into the churchyard wall records the lighting of the town by gas in 1832, and a commemorative column in Bath Road acknowledges the gift of the lamp columns to the town by Admiral Sir Harry Neale. The townspeople were obviously gratified to have street lighting, but it was not a new invention then. Most of the West End of London was lit in 1816 and Southampton in 1820.

Old brick garden walls were sometimes built in serpentine fashion, ie curving in and out. They provided more sunshine for fruit trees and did not need to be as thick as normal walls or need buttresses. They were most common in Suffolk and Hampshire and were known as 'crinkle-crankle' walls. There are a few in Lymington; two are in Church Lane and another is at the rear of No. 73 High Street (it can be seen from School Lane). One of those in Church Lane is the wall of Grove Place, a house now demolished that was the home of Dennis Wheatley, the famous writer of occult thrillers.

St Thomas's church has three interesting memorials in the chancel. The one to Matthew Blakiston (1806) reads: 'To those who knew him the enumeration of his virtues would be superfluous. To those who knew him not it might be tedious'. The memorial to Josias Rogers (1795) is a very fine example of the type common in the period 1760–1830, that of a female figure standing by an urn. The one to Charles Colborne (1747) is by the famous sculptor Rysbrack.

A gravestone in the churchyard near the chancel reads:

Pray move not for I intend hear to ly untel the end
Hear lyeth the bodey of Ios . . . kilton . . .

Also in the churchyard is the tomb of Caroline Bowles, second wife of the poet Robert Southey and a poet in her own right. She returned to Buckland near Lymington after his death.

General James Wolfe spent his last night in England at No. 15 High Street (now The Stanwell House Hotel) before leaving next day for Canada.

Lymington is 'twinned' with Vitré, an ancient town in Brittany with medieval houses and a castle.

Lyndhurst

➤ Lyndhurst means 'lime tree wood', an interesting derivation because there are not many lime trees in the vicinity today. Of the many shops in the village one in particular catches the eye – the butcher's shop of John Strange. If you would like to try venison this is the place to buy it – you can even get venison sausages there. Before cooking venison it should be hung in a dry place for between seven and ten days.

Two periods of ecclesiastical architecture are predominant in Hampshire – the Transitional (Norman to Early English) and the Victorian. St Michael and All Angels at Lyndhurst is a notable example of the latter period. It was designed by William White, who in his early years worked under George Gilbert Scott and later, as here at Lyndhurst, demonstrated that a talented Victorian architect could produce a design of exceptional merit. The outstanding feature in the church is the fresco painted by Frederick Leighton, said to be the first in an English church since the Reformation. It depicts the parable of the wise and foolish virgins, and the models were all local girls. How many volunteered for each category is not known!

The Jennings memorial in the church was executed by the famous sculptor Flaxman, who made the designs for the white figures on Wedgwood pottery. In the churchyard is buried Mrs Alice Hargreaves, who as Alice Liddell was the subject of Lewis Carroll's *Alice's Adventures in Wonderland*. The Hargreaves lived at Cuffnell's, a house near Lyndhurst (now demolished). A memorial to their two sons, killed in the First World War, is in the church.

Marchwood

The name Marchwood means 'the wood where smallage grows'; smallage (a word now obsolete) was wild celery or parsley.

Follow the road from the village to Cracknore Hard, ignoring the industrial and defence establishments on the way, until you arrive at a tiny public car park on the bank of the river Test. There is room only for about five cars and it is the only spot between Hythe pier and Eling with access to the river. Across the river are Southampton Docks, and you have a splendid view of ships passing up and down. The only pastime expressly forbidden on the hard is digging for bait! There was once a ferry from Cracknore Hard to Town Quay, Southampton.

Near the parish church is a large semi-circular brick memorial to ten men of the Royal Fleet Auxiliary who lost their lives in three different ships in defence of the Falkland Islands in

Cracknore Hard near Marchwood

1982. The memorial is tastefully ornamented with insignia and makes a fitting tribute. A separate block of stone has a plaque with an engraving of one of the ships.

Martin

➤ Martin Down in the far north-west corner of Hampshire is a National Nature Reserve of considerable importance, yet it is relatively little known because of its remoteness. Its interest lies in its great variety of downland habitats and its range of chalk grassland species; its successful maintenance depends on constant grazing by sheep. Types of scrub found on the down include hawthorn, dogwood, elder and gorse, which provide cover for animals such as roe deer and brown hares and a wide variety of birds and butterflies.

In addition to its natural history interest Martin Down has a greater number and variety of prehistoric earthworks than any comparable area in Hampshire, these again being little known yet of national importance. Bokerley Ditch, the longest and most impressive earthwork in the county, is a four-mile-long bank and ditch running in a sinuous course along the county boundary; in places it is 100 ft wide and 15 ft high. It was constructed in three phases by the Romano-British in the 4th century AD as a defensive boundary bank facing north-east, the direction from which invaders were expected. It closed a gap between two areas of woodland and must have been as daunting a sight then as it is now.

In contrast Grim's Ditch, long stretches of which survive on the downs, is a system of smaller banks and ditches that followed a meandering course and enclosed some 14 square miles. The purpose of these banks and ditches can only be surmised, but they were probably land boundaries or enclosures that evolved over a long period during the Bronze Age and the Iron Age. They may well be the earliest large-scale land divisions in Europe.

The track opposite the car park on the A354 crosses the Roman road from Old Sarum to Badbury Rings. Here the road, or agger as it is called, forms a well-preserved embankment. It is thought that the reason for making the agger so prominent here (unnecessarily so compared with other Roman roads) was to impress the native population. A little further on is a good example of a long barrow, a type of prehistoric burial mound; it is wider at its south-east end where the burials were made. Long barrows were peculiar to the neolithic period and were usually reserved for important families.

A short distance to the west of this barrow, at the edge of the wood, is the westernmost point in Hampshire, which is about 56 miles as the crow flies from the easternmost point at Aldershot. Half a mile north of the barrow, at the very edge of the wood, is the point where the boundaries of Hampshire, Dorset and Wiltshire meet.

Until 1895 the parish of Martin was in Wiltshire, and it still has more affinity with that county than with Hampshire. The village has changed little over the centuries and there is little traffic to disturb its rural peace; it is too remote to have suffered any development. An attractive village, Martin also has a peculiar fascination, so well described by W. H. Hudson in his book *A Shepherd's Life*. He called it 'Winterbourne Bishop' and described the village street and its people with loving care. In the churchyard is the grave of William Lawes, who died in 1886 at the age of 86; he was the original of 'Isaac Bawcombe', one of the characters in the book. The Allen river used to cascade down the village street in winter, but now it goes underground through a culvert. John Aubrey, the antiquary, wrote: 'I take Martin to be the best seated for healthy airs etc and sports of any place in the county' (ie Wiltshire).

The stages in the growth of the village can be deduced from its buildings: the houses of the 15th century, eg The Priest's House and Hart House (formerly the White Hart inn), the 16th-entury manor house, the half-timbered cottages of the 17th century, eg Simmys, Harris Farm and Yew Tree Cottage (dated 1653), the red-brick farmhouses of the 18th century, eg Williams Farm House, and the chapel of 1829. It is thought that the timber used in the older houses was from broken-up ships, brought from Poole by the cart-load.

On the village green, near the remains of the old cross, is a rusty but rather splendid old hand-pump. It has an iron frame with a cranked spindle and a flywheel. Until 1921 this pump was the only source of water for the local farmers and householders.

The old coach road from Salisbury to Poole followed the track over Toyd Down, through the hamlet of Tidpit, up over Tidpit Down and Blackheath Down, and through Martin Wood to Cranborne. One of the old milestones, in remarkable condition for its 200 years, stands by the roadside at Blackheath Down. Its inscription reads: 'XIX miles from Poole Gate III miles from Cranborn'.

In 1818 the road from Poole was improved as far as Tidpit but not beyond; it was eventually superseded by what is now the A354. The old road is shown in John Ogilby's *Britannia* of 1675; he shows a windmill on the wooded hill near Tidpit that is now named Windmill Hill, and he calls the hamlet of Tidpit 'Tippit'.

Mattingley

➤ The bus shelter on the A33 at Mattingley is also a war memorial – a combination probably unique in Hampshire, and a reminder that there have been much greater hardships than waiting for a bus. The shelter is ornamented with delicate wrought-iron tracery, and the names of the war victims are carved on a wooden plaque.

The shelter stands near Mattingley Green, which is not really a green because it is covered with a dense growth of trees and scrub. Hazeley Heath on the other hand really is a heath, a large area of common land with old overgrown pits that produced clay for the local brickmaking industry. Common rights were abolished in the 19th century and the public have access only for air and exercise.

Mattingley church is of unusual construction; the walls are timber-framed and the infilling between the timbers is brick-nogging. Old wattle-and-daub and lath-and-plaster infillings in house walls were often replaced by brick from the 17th century onwards. The date of the brickwork here is not known; the bricks are set in herring-bone style, ie obliquely, to form an attractive zigzag pattern. The church was once a chapel-of-ease of St Michael's church at Heckfield, which is probably why it has no dedication.

Meonstoke

➤ Very rarely has a church changed its dedication, but in 1830 Meonstoke was changed from St Mary to St Andrew. The list of rectors contains a large number of high-ranking ecclesiastics because the combined living of Soberton and Meonstoke produced a considerable income, and pluralism being a common practice the rectors found it profitable to employ a vicar or curate to carry out their duties for them.

The church, the river, and the large private garden in front of the church make an attractive picture. In the village there are many interesting old houses and cottages in High Street, which runs parallel to the river.

The name of the village and the river is derived from the Meonware tribe, who were Jutish settlers of the post-Roman period. In 1972 a 6th-century Anglo-Saxon grave was discovered; it contained human bones and various grave goods, including an iron spear-head and a knife.

Micheldever

The origin of the first part of the name Micheldever is obscure; the second part means 'water', referring to the little river Dever, which rises in Stratton Park and meets the Test at Wherwell. The village seems to have grown up at the junction of two old trackways or drove roads, one from Overton to Winchester, the other from Stockbridge to Alton.

There are so many superb old black-and-white timber-framed cottages in Micheldever that it is rather invidious to name any, but among the best are Bluebell Cottage, The Old Cottage, Perry's Acre and The Old Post Office. Most of the Victorian and modern houses in the village remain discreetly in the background, but one that does not is a building near the church that has been derelict for years. It has a genuine old bow-windowed shop-front with an advertisement for Wills's Wild Woodbines.

St Mary's church is one of the oddest in Hampshire for when it was restored in 1808–9 a brick octagonal nave was inserted into the medieval church. The result is startling for its audacity rather than for its beauty or its architectural quality. The architect, George Dance junior, had done something similar in London at St Bartholomew the Less, which was also given a centrally-planned nave. Dance was a classical though unorthodox architect of great originality, and was not afraid to experiment as he did here. There is no record of what the villagers thought when it was finished! The old tower of 1527 was retained in the restoration.

The three monuments to the Baring family by the famous sculptor Flaxman date from 1801 to 1813. They display Baroque influence in their details – very late examples of this style. Sir Francis Baring, founder of the banking firm, lies under the chancel. His life-long deafness apparently did not hinder his successful financial career – it may even have been an asset!

In an unmarked grave lies the Marquis de Ruvigny, a French Huguenot who became a general in the British army and commander at many great battles. He died here in 1720. Also in an unmarked grave lies Henry Cook, hanged in 1830 at the age of 19 for knocking off a Justice's hat (with a sledgehammer) in a local riot. The charge for this offence was attempted murder. That same Justice, William Baring, the son of the millionaire banker, himself beat a handcuffed but innocent prisoner with a stick in cold blood, for which brutal attack he had to pay damages of £50. One law for the rich and one law for the poor in 1830.

Nearly 2½ miles north of the village is Micheldever station still, as in 1840 when it was built, the only station on the 19-mile stretch of railway between Winchester and Basingstoke. Alone of the early station buildings on the London to Southampton line it remains virtually unaltered. It was named Andover Road until 1856, because it was the nearest station to Andover until the latter acquired its own station in 1854. The architect was Sir William Tite, who also designed the station buildings at Winchester, Southampton Terminus and Gosport. It is a simple flint-faced building with tall chimneys and a veranda, slightly Italianate in appearance.

On 11th May 1840 a great celebration was held at Andover Road station to mark the opening of the completed London to Southampton line. Thousands of people arrived from all parts of the county and spacious marquees were erected at Warren Farm. On the flat roof of the station colonnade the Hurstbourne brass band played a variety of lively pieces in a 'scientific manner' (whatever that means!). Each train was greeted with artillery salvoes. Five hundred invited guests were treated to a cold lunch and an unlimited supply of champagne, claret and other wines, and the workers feasted on roast ox and strong beer, with which they 'made themselves merry', according to the *Hampshire Chronicle*. Micheldever had never before been so noisy, and has not been so noisy since!

Micheldever Wood, now cut through by the M3 motorway, has been in the care of the Forestry Commission since 1927. It contains large areas of beech and oak planted 60 years ago. Part of it is a wild life reserve; three species of deer roam here and butterflies in particular abound. For walkers there are tracks and a waymarked path. Many remains of early settlement have been found in the wood – Bronze Age, Iron Age and Roman – and it is probable that many more will eventually come to light.

Michelmersh

➤ St Mary's church, with its unusual 15th-century detached wooden bell-tower, has three interesting memorials. The most prominent is the cross-legged effigy of a Crusader knight of about 1320; the stag at his feet suggests that he may have been a King's Forester. The tablet that commemorates Trustram Fantleroy and his wife (1538) is probably the earliest example in Hampshire of a memorial with detached kneeling figures, a type that was introduced in the first half of the 16th century. The third memorial is to General Sir William Ogle, who defended Winchester Castle against Cromwell in 1645. His ghost is said to gallop on horseback through the village – yet nobody has ever seen it!

The field immediately south of the church is said to have been the scene of an historic event in 1415. More than 600 knights and archers are supposed to have camped there before sailing to France and the Battle of Agincourt, and to have been reviewed by the Duke of Gloucester. Whatever the truth of the story, the field is known as Agincourt Field.

Opposite the church, on the left of the farm buildings at Old Michelmersh Farm, is a very old and unusual five-bayed weatherboarded granary, said to be the largest of its type in Hampshire. Like most Hampshire granaries it has a hipped and tiled roof and rests on staddle-stones. It was here that the television film *Worzel Gummidge*, starring Jon Pertwee, was made.

On the Romsey to Stockbridge road is the Bear and Ragged Staff inn; this name is not so unusual as one might think. The signboard depicts the coat of arms of the Earls of Warwick with their motto incorrectly reading: 'Vix ea nostra vox' – 'vox' should be 'voco' ('I scarcely call these things our own'). It seems that the first Earl was known as the 'Bear' for having strangled one single-handed, and another earl, not to be outdone, slew a giant with a tree-shaped club, hence the 'Bear and Ragged Staff'.

Timsbury was named Timbreberie in Domesday Book, the

name probably meaning 'fort made of timber', perhaps the predecessor of the manor house.

The ancient church of St Andrew at Timsbury is really hidden away; perhaps that is why it largely escaped Victorian restoration and remains one of the best little churches in the county. It has one of the only two sets of 14th-century pews in Hampshire, one of the few pre-Reformation chancel screens and a pulpit with the inscription 'Wo is unto me if I preach not ye gospel'. You may have to collect the key from the vicar to get in the church.

Timsbury, small as it is, has a 'twin' – Ryes in Normandy, a village two miles south of Arromanches on the coast, where a Mulberry harbour enabled the Allied forces to land in 1944.

Milford on Sea

➤ The expansion of the village began in 1866–7, when Colonel Cornwallis-West of Newlands Manor devised a scheme to make it the Eastbourne of Hampshire. This fortunately perhaps did not happen, only pleasure gardens, roads and a hotel being built; the village then became known as Milford on Sea. The mill in the name Milford was mentioned in Domesday Book.

At the corner of Cornwallis Road and Victoria Road stands the oldest pillar-box in Hampshire, one of the 20 oldest in the country. It dates from about 1856, and has vertical fluting and a vertical posting slot. Its site is rather curious, for at that date there were no houses or roads in that part of Milford. It was probably moved there from elsewhere at some time in the next 40 years because it is shown on the 1896 Ordnance Survey map. (For another early pillar-box see Denmead.)

On the north side of the churchyard close to All Saints church there are two flat gravestones lying north-south instead of the customary east-west. They are said to be the graves of two suicides; this may have been the traditional method of differentiating them from those who died from more natural causes. One inscription is unreadable, and the legible part of the other one reads: 'William Greer . . . After witnessing the departure of all that was most dear to him, of a wife and many daughters, he departed himself from this world. . . . in the 87th year of his age.' It is said that the words 'he departed himself' indicate suicide, but it might just be bad grammar for 'he himself departed'.

Look at the two grotesque carved heads above the window of the south aisle of the church. One is of a man playing a sort of bagpipe, the other of a man wearing ear-pads!

West of the village, near Hordle House, is the graveyard of old Hordle church, deserted since 1830. Dozens of gravestones, once completely overgrown but now open to view, lie around the site of the church. Some of the graves are of people washed ashore from shipwrecks, such as the *British Tar*, which foundered on these cliffs in 1818 with a cargo of wood and ivory.

Minstead

In its wealth of old furniture and fittings All Saints church is surpassed only by St Mary's at Whitby, North Yorkshire. The squire's pew even has a large fireplace – the gentry kept warm in the winter while the common folk shivered in the south transept or up in the galleries.

The font stands in an unusual place – directly below the three-decker pulpit. The traditional place for fonts is at the west end near the entrance, as a symbol of a person's entrance into the Church by baptism. In the 17th century the church authorities agreed to allow fonts to be moved to the front of those churches where it was difficult for the congregation to see and hear the baptism service. With few exceptions, Minstead being one, fonts have been moved back to the west end.

On the west side of the churchyard is the grave of Thomas Maynard, who died in 1807 at the age of 27. He was a member of the Band of Musicians of the South Hants Yeomanry and his headstone has a carving of the old musical instrument known as a serpent, an essential part of church bands in those days.

On the north side is the grave of Thomas White, whose epitaph reads:

A faithful friend. A father dear.
A —— husband lies buried here.
In love he lived. In love he died.
His life we craved, but God denied.

The missing word is probably 'faithful'. White's widow sus-
pected her husband's infidelity and deciding that the truth
must prevail had the word removed.

The man who was buried at the far south end of the churchyard should have written about that under the title: 'The Case
of the Missing Word'. He was Arthur Conan Doyle, creator of
Sherlock Holmes, who lived at Bignell House in Minstead. He
died in Sussex in 1930 but was reburied here. His gravestone
reads:

STEEL TRUE
BLADE STRAIGHT
ARTHUR CONAN DOYLE
KNIGHT
PATRIOT, PHYSICIAN & MAN OF LETTERS

Minstead featured in his book *The White Company*.

The name of the Trusty Servant Inn requires some explanation. The original of the picture on the signboard hangs in
Winchester College and dates from about 1600. It shows a man
with stag's feet, pig's snout and ass's ears, the significance of
which is explained by the verse underneath. Near the inn is the
old Minstead Technical College of 1897, now known as Crofton
Cottages.

A route through the forest that passes several little-known
sights (and one or two well-known ones) starts on the road from
Emery Down to Bolderwood. Beyond Millyford Bridge on the
left is the Portuguese Fireplace, a relic of the camp that was
occupied by a Portuguese Army unit in the First World War. At
the Deer Sanctuary at Bolderwood you may see deer at feeding
time, but at other times you are just as likely to see them in the
recesses of the forest as here. Deer have lived in the New Forest
since it became a hunting park. An Act of 1851 ordered the
removal of all deer in the forest, but a few hundred survived.

Portuguese Fireplace, Minstead

Today there are five species of deer in the forest – fallow, red, roe, sika and muntjac – and the total number is about 1,500. The Radnor Stone near the Deer Sanctuary commemorates the Earl of Radnor and has engravings of birds, insects and plants of the New Forest.

The Bolderwood Ornamental Drive leads south to the well-known Knightwood Oak, an example of a pollarded oak nearly 400 years old and one of the largest trees in the forest. It is in The Monarch's Grove (should not the sign read The Monarchs' Grove?) where 18 oak trees have been planted to commemorate all the recorded visits to the New Forest by reigning monarchs from William I to Edward VII. There is a 19th outside the grove, known as the Queen's Oak, planted by the Queen in 1979 to mark the 9th centenary of the founding of the New Forest.

Near the Queen's Oak there is an example of 'inosculation', where the branches of two adjoining trees unite. It is quite common for this to happen with trees of the same species, but here is a most unusual case of an oak and a beech taking a fancy to each other. Lastly the Eagle Oak in Knightwood Enclosure, which is right in the forest and may take some finding, is said to be the spot where the last white eagle was shot in 1810.

At Barrow Moor car park on the Ornamental Drive you are really in the heart of the New Forest, for this is the furthest you can get from any point of the forest boundary, and appropriately enough it is one of the most beautiful spots.

Monk Sherborne

➤ The *Hampshire Treasures Survey* describes Monk Sherborne Wood as a place of great beauty, secluded and unfrequented. Beautiful it may be, secluded and unfrequented it certainly is because it is strictly private, so beware!

A secluded place that you may visit however, by following a track past Kiln Green, which is not far from The Mole public house, is known locally as Rookery Dell. Used by local people for over 100 years, this enormous old chalk-pit is overgrown with wild plants and surrounded by beech trees. Not exactly beautiful, but wild and uncannily quiet, it is an oasis in a modern arable desert; a more hidden place in Hampshire it would be hard to find.

The *Monk* in the village name comes from the Benedictine priory that was here, part of the church of which survives (known as Pamber Priory). It is used as the parish church of Pamber, though it is in fact in Monk Sherborne parish. Only the chancel and the crossing tower of the priory church remain, the nave having been destroyed when the priory was dissolved in 1414.

In 1462 the church was granted to St Julian's (God's House) in Southampton, which belongs to Queen's College, Oxford; the College therefore owns Pamber church. The 15th-century benches and screen are evidently part of the refurnishing of the church after its dissolution.

The Cross was the dominant motif on early carved coffin-lids and examples of its use can be seen on the 12th-century coffin-lids in the church. The wooden effigy of a knight of about 1310 also repays examination.

Monk Sherborne parish church is also worth a visit, if only to see the 14th-century wooden porch. The door is of about the same age too, and the benches and pulpit are of the 17th century.

A brass tablet records that Thomas Sympson in 1674 left to the poor of six parishes the sum of £15 every year 'so long as the world shall endure'. Let's hope there is enough money in the kitty! There are similar tablets in all six churches.

Of the many fine houses and cottages in the village perhaps the best is Queens Meadow, thatched and timber-framed, which proudly displays its date of 1375, though it has been refronted since then.

Morestead

➤ In the Middle Ages travellers from London to Southampton did not have to go via Winchester as they do today. From Alresford the direct road went over Cheesefoot Head and Fawley Down and through Morestead and Twyford. It was in fact Winchester's first bypass!

It is uncertain when this route superseded the older route via the Itchen valley and Winchester but it must have been after the foundation of New Alresford in 1200. The road is shown in John Ogilby's atlas *Britannia* (1675) as 'The road from London to Southampton'. It can still be followed as a series of lanes and footpaths, and makes a delightful and invigorating walk.

The little Norman church at Morestead is of simple nave-and-chancel design; the nave windows and the chancel are Victorian. The church has no known dedication.

Mortimer West End

➤ Here is the northernmost point in Hampshire, on the road that passes Gibbet Piece. At this spot you are 51 miles as the crow flies from Hurst Castle, the southernmost point. That may seem a long way, but Hampshire is the ninth largest English county in size.

The dead-straight east-west road through the parish is named Welshman's Road, a reminder of the Welsh drovers who used it. At the western end of this road, almost on the Berkshire boundary, you will find a disused chapel built about 1800 for the Countess of Huntingdon's Connexion, who were followers of George Whitefield and his Methodists. Most of their chapels later became Congregational.

The amphitheatre of the Roman town of Calleva (Silchester) is in the extreme south of the parish, just outside the wall of the Roman town and not far from Silchester parish church; many visitors miss it through not knowing where it is. It has recently been drained, cleaned and excavated, so that its plan is now clear. Above the surrounding stone wall there would once have been wooden seats to accommodate about 4,000 spectators. Here the citizens held their contests and barbaric games, an entertainment comparable to our football matches, and the spectators were no doubt almost as noisy and unruly.

Mottisfont

By the late 18th or early 19th century most large country houses had an ice-house in their grounds. It was built of brick or stone, conical or circular, usually underground, and covered with earth and grass. The ice, collected locally in the winter would keep for about a year. The need for ice-houses disappeared with the advent of ice-making machines and refrigerators. There are remains of over 40 ice-houses in Hampshire, but only a few are in good condition; their shape and size vary considerably. An ice-house can be seen just beyond the new graveyard south of Mottisfont church, in an overgrown chalk-pit. There is another one, which visitors can enter, in the grounds of Mottisfont Abbey.

St Andrew's church has more 15th-century stained glass than any other Hampshire church; it includes a Crucifixion in the east window. Other notable features of the church include a fine Norman chancel arch with zigzag and billet decoration, a bell-tower supported by six timber posts, and a rare 17th-century clock movement. The monument of 1584 to an unknown Elizabethan family has kneeling figures and Renaissance decoration.

Nately Scures

➤ The little church of St Swithun, standing next to a farmhouse alongside the A30, is one of the only three Norman single-celled aisleless apsidal churches in England. (The other two are at North Marden, West Sussex, and Little Tey, Essex.) It is the smallest church still in use in Hampshire.

The only entrance is on the north side, which is unusual (but see Greywell). The memorials are almost entirely of the Carletons; one was a Governor-General of Canada and another was one of the longest-living survivors of the Battle of Trafalgar. Four of the memorial tablets, dating from 1892 to 1963, are in the shape of the suits of a pack of cards. There is no obvious reason for this touch of macabre humour; perhaps the family was famous for its skill at cards!

A carving of a mermaid on the doorway has given rise to a local legend, in which it is said that a sailor jilted a mermaid in some distant ocean, returned to England and was about to marry a girl in this church when the mermaid appeared and carried him off to sea again – a warning to flirtatious men!

Nately Scures is shown on the 1817 Ordnance Survey map as 'Skewers', a quaint corruption of the name. Roger de Scures was the owner of the manor in the 13th century.

Nether Wallop

➤ Wallop means simply 'valley of the stream', disappointingly prosaic perhaps but obvious when you know that the village follows the course of the Wallop brook for a mile and a quarter. It has a well-deserved reputation for its beautiful old cottages; together with its neighbour Over Wallop upstream there are few equals in Hampshire. The cottages remain but times change; in and around The Square there were five shops as recently as 1960, but now there is only one – The Trout Wine Shop, the descendant of an ancient ale-house.

The pair of cottages dated 1861 near the bridge were built to the published designs of architect Henry Roberts on behalf of the Society for Improving the Condition of the Labouring Classes. Thousands of houses based on his designs were built in England; they were well-constructed and cheap (about £150 each) and well in advance of their time. It would be no exaggeration to say that Roberts changed the face of Victorian rural England.

At the very south end of the village are the mill, which until 1949 produced feed for game birds (see the inscription high up on the wall), and Place (formerly Place Farm House), once the home of the conductor Leopold Stokowski.

St Andrew's church has the most remarkable set of wall-paintings in Hampshire. Above the chancel arch, and partly destroyed by it, is a figure of Christ in Majesty supported by flying angels. It is most probably the work of the Winchester School of artists in the late 10th or early 11th century, and it may be the only Saxon wall-painting in England in its original position. Christ in Majesty was a common subject above chancel arches before the Doom or Last Judgement later became popular.

On the south wall of the nave is a rare 15th-century morality painting, a warning to sabbath-breakers. It depicts the body of Christ wounded by the tools and implements commonly in use in the Middle Ages, illustrating the result of working on a Sunday. On the west wall is a unique painting of a large bell, which may commemorate the hanging of the first bell in the church in 1585. The church has five bells, as might be guessed by the name of the local public house.

In the churchyard is the strange 15-foot-high pyramidal tomb of Dr Francis Douce (died 1760). He left money in his will 'that the boys and girls of the parish are taught to read and write and cast an account a little way, but they must not go too far least it makes them saucy and the girls all want to be chamber maids, and in a few years you will be in want of cooks'. He also stipulated that the railings round his tomb should be painted every second year, but they have at some time been removed, which is perhaps why his ghost has been seen walking round and round the tomb!

Erecting pyramids seems to have been a family trait. His cousin Paulet St John built the well-known memorial on Farley Mount and another relative, 'Mad' Jack Fuller, built himself a pyramidal tomb at Brightling in East Sussex.

Netley

➤ Netley is in the parish of Hound (Old English *hune* meaning 'hoarhound'), and the little parish church of St Mary stands well away from Netley village. It escaped restoration and enlargement when a large new church was built at Netley in 1886. Though almost entirely of the Early English period its most memorable feature is the modern stained glass east window by Patrick Reyntiens. The figures represent the Virgin and Child and are almost abstract in design, but the colouring helps to make it a masterful composition.

St Edward's church at Netley has a medieval effigy of a crusader-monk, which came from the ruins of Netley Abbey and was formerly built into the wall of Netley Castle. The churchyard displays a notice 'Danger to dogs' but from what they are in danger is not specified. A good way to keep the dogs and their owners out anyway.

The older part of Netley village is pure Victorian, with typical villas and terraced houses. There was nothing here until the Royal Victoria Hospital (1856–63) and the railway (1866) were built. The railway station building is a good period piece, simple classical in the L&SWR tradition.

New Alresford

➤ New Alresford is not really very new; it was created by Bishop de Lucy in about 1200 as one of his six 'planned' towns; it was at first called Novum Forum or New Market. From its very beginning it had a market and a fair, and must have been a sound financial proposition to the Bishop by means of rents from building plots.

In the early 18th century Daniel Defoe wrote that Alresford was remarkable because 'though it had no great trade and little if any manufactures, yet there was no collection in the town for the poor, nor any poor enough to take alms', which could not in his opinion be said of any other town in England. This happy state of affairs was brought to an end by a 'sudden and surprising fire' (the great fire of 1689, which destroyed 117 houses). New Alresford has very little poverty today either, to judge by its many antique and craft shops and flourishing inns. If Defoe were to return he would probably come to the same conclusion.

The parish church, rebuilt in 1898, is a good example of the Perpendicular style of the Gothic Revival. On the west face of the tower is a tiny Saxon crucifix, but the oldest objects (and probably the oldest in any Hampshire church) are two inscribed stones, one dating from about 2150 BC from the Ziggurat at Ur, the other of 604–562 BC from Babylon.

A 17th-century vicar was Peter Heylyn (or Heylin), a well-known historian and theologian of his day. A royalist, he was deposed in 1640; reinstated in 1661, he died a year later. His works include a survey of France and a history of the Reformation.

Most of the buildings in New Alresford date from after the great fire of 1689; many are of the 18th century. Broad Street is rated by many people Hampshire's most attractive street, its rivals being The Square at Wickham, High Street, Odiham and High Street, Fareham.

No house in Broad Street stands out, but note No. 27, the birthplace of the novelist Mary Russell Mitford, No. 23 The Old Post House and No. 47, five-bayed and 17th century in date. Wykeham House in Mill Hill, at the bottom of Broad Street, has an old sundial on the wall. East Street displays a galaxy of old bow-windowed fronts; perhaps the best is the five-bayed No. 6 with its fine doorway. The Old Sun was formerly an inn and was once the home of the cricket writer John Arlott. In West Street the building now Nos. 56–60 was until 1932 Perin's Grammar School, founded in 1697.

New Alresford is 'twinned' with Bricquebec, an ancient town south of Cherbourg in Normandy that has a 14th-century castle and a Trappist monastery.

New Milton

➤ Old Milton village centre is just about recognisable, though there are few buildings of any great age still standing. Around the green the parish church, The George Inn (1905), the bow-windowed Myrtle Cottage and the thatched cottage adjoining it were once part of the old village scene.

When the railway arrived in 1888 a new shopping centre grew up near the station, which was a mile north of the old village. The new post office and then the station used the prefix 'New' and so New Milton was born. It became a town in 1979.

The station building is dated 'AD 1886'. Why it was thought necessary to add 'AD' is a mystery. The railway opened on 6th March 1888, so the station building must have been completed in good time.

The most prominent building in the town, the enormous water-tower of 1900, is also the ugliest. It even makes the mediocre post-war buildings in the town seem quite acceptable in comparison.

North Hayling

➤ The first bridge connecting the mainland to Hayling Island was opened in 1824, when development of the island was planned; before that there was a ford, passable at low tide, known as the 'Wadeway' or 'Horse road to low water'. The bridge had a toll and was replaced in 1956 by the present bridge, which was then the longest pre-stressed concrete bridge in England. The toll continued until 1960; those exempt from it included the royal family, the mail service and the armed services. The toll for a pedestrian was always a half-penny and for a hearse (with or without its corpse) always two shillings and six pence.

The Hayling Island Railway was opened in 1867, crossing to the island from Havant over a wooden bridge, the remains of which can be seen from the road bridge or at close quarters by walking to it along the old railway. Before the days of motor cars and buses the railway was the chief means of communication with the island; the little tank locomotives used on the line were affectionately known as 'Hayling Billys'. The line closed in 1963.

St Peter's, with its shingled steeple, is a homely little 12th and 13th-century church. It has two ancient pews, the poppy-heads of which have holes for candles. Outside is the grave of Princess Yourievsky, a member of the Russian royal family.

The old railway bridge at North Hayling

Nursling

The earliest form of the name Nursling was Nhutscelle (in an 8th-century life of St Boniface), in Domesday Book it was Notesselinge, and on the early Ordnance Survey map it was Nutshalling. The Old English word *hnutscelle* meaning 'nutshell' was a strange name to give to a settlement or a monastery but it may have been given as a joke because it was such a tiny place.

Small though it is Nursling has in the last 200 years found itself in a vulnerable position for transport routes. The Andover Canal and then the Andover and Redbridge Railway were constructed through the village, and now it is afflicted by not one but two motorways.

The Andover Canal was opened in 1794; it was used to carry coal and building materials from Southampton to Romsey and Andover and to carry agricultural products the other way. It was closed in 1859, the canal company never having paid a dividend on its shares. The Andover and Redbridge Railway, built over the old canal bed for much of the way, was opened in 1865. It was known as the 'sprat and winkle' line probably because Andover people could buy fresh fish from Southampton for the first time.

The canal survives in several places between Timsbury and Redbridge. At Nursling it can best be seen alongside the railway in the bridge near Station House. There is no longer a station in Nursling; the house has the prominent date AD 1883 (that superfluous 'AD' again!).

Nursling is 'twinned' with Percy, which you might think was a person rather than a place in Normandy, and you would not be far wrong because the Dukes of Northumberland, whose family name is Percy, originate from there.

Nursing church is dedicated to St Boniface, the Apostle of Germany. St Boniface, or Winfrid to give him his real name, came from Devon to the Benedictine monastery at Nursling (the site is not known). He spent the last 36 years of his life (he died in AD 755) converting people to Christianity in Germany. Sir Arthur Bryant, the historian, wrote that no Englishman has ever had a greater influence on European history than St Boniface.

Andrew Mundy (died 1632) is commemorated in the church by three brasses. One of them has a punning reference to his name in the form of a chronogram: 'LeX aeternI LVX MVnDI' (Law eternal, Light of the world). The letters in capitals are also roman numerals and add up to 1632. A second brass has another chronogram: 'Vt CererI fVnVs aC phoenICI CInIs Vesper apoLLini sIC MIhI fInIs' (As death was to Ceres, ashes to the phoenix, and evening to Apollo, so is my end to me). The roman numerals again add up to 1632. The third brass reads 'Nec zenith nec nadir' (Neither the peak nor the lowest point).

The well-preserved Nursling Mill on the river Test has an inscribed stone set into its wall that reads: 'This Building stands on a Frame of Large Beech Timber which was given by Sr RICHd MILL BARtt in Memory of whose kindness this Stone was placed here by H K 1728'. 'H K' was presumably Henry Knollys who lived at Grove Place.

Grove Place, which can be seen at the end of its drive, is an Elizabethan mansion now housing a preparatory school. In the 1950s it was offered for sale with its 15 bedrooms, long gallery, Tudor panelling and twelve acres of grounds, with vacant possession, for £9,500.

Odiham

At the time of Domesday Book Odiham was a large and important place; it had eight mills and four churches, and its population of 247 was the second largest in Hampshire (after Winchester). There was also a royal palace, which was superseded by the castle at North Warnborough. The English Parliament met at Odiham in 1303. With its historic past one might think that Odiham would have adopted town status, but it seems happy with its Parish Council.

The street plan and many of the buildings have remained unchanged since medieval times. A map of 1739 shows two or three buildings in the middle of High Street, one of them being the market house, opposite The George inn. Though at first sight High Street appears to consist predominantly of Georgian houses many of them in fact have refaced fronts and the side walls reveal their medieval timber-framing. High Street can stand comparison with any village street in Hampshire for its wealth of architecture, and fortunately the whole of medieval Odiham has been designated a Conservation Area.

In The Bury, the open space in front of the church, are the old stocks and whipping-post; they are among the very few surviving in the county. Stocks were introduced to 'encourage virtue and discourage evil doers' and were in use from the 14th century to the early 19th century. An act of 1405 decreed that every town and village should have a set; so important were they thought to be that a village was not considered worthy of the name unless it had a set. The parish in those days had more control over local affairs, and the Petty Constable or a Justice of the Peace could set a person in the stocks for drunkenness and other offences (what a good idea, did you say?). The stocks were no doubt uncomfortable, but the whipping-post, which appeared on the scene in about 1600, was quite another matter.

Behind the church, near the almshouses of 1623, is the pest house of about the same date. This was used to house local inhabitants suffering from the plague and kindred diseases, to keep them isolated from other people. Here they stayed until they recovered or died; the siting of the pest house on the edge of the churchyard may therefore have been deliberate. Not many pest houses have survived; this is one of the few in Hampshire. It has its original fireplace and bread oven, and was used as a house from 1780 to 1930. It is now a small museum open at certain times.

All Saints church has a large number of old brasses, the earliest being of 1400. Other interesting objects include a map of 1739 showing the streets and houses of Odiham in some detail, and a hudd or vicar's shelter, which resembles a sentry-box and was used at graveside services in bad weather so that however wet the mourners became the vicar at least remained dry!

A short distance from North Warnborough village and best approached along the canal tow-path is the ruined keep of Odiham Castle, built in 1207–14 for King John. It is one of the only two octagonal keeps in England (the other is at

Chilham, Kent). The castle was conveniently situated between Winchester and Windsor, with hunting available in the nearby park; King John stayed many times and was here the night before he set out to Runnymede to seal Magna Carta. David Bruce, King of Scotland, was imprisoned here for two years. The castle became dilapidated in the 15th century and only the keep survives as mute testimony to royal power in the Middle Ages.

In London Road, a mile from Odiham, there is a milestone of 1736 inscribed 'London 40 miles'. But from this point to the City of London it is only 40 miles as the crow flies, so it must be more than that by road. The answer to this puzzle must be that the mileage was computed in 'customary' miles, which varied in length in different parts of England; here the 'customary' mile was longer than the statute mile, which was not then in general use.

Old Alresford

➤ Old Alresford Pond dates from about 1200 when The Great Weir, an enormous dam, was constructed. It had always been thought that the pond was made as a reservoir to supply water to a canal that linked Alresford with Winchester via the rivers Alre and Itchen. It has recently been proved that without much doubt there never was a canal or navigation and the huge pond was in fact a fishpond that also supplied water to the three Alresford mills.

Admiral Lord Rodney is buried in St Mary's church, in the family vault in the chancel. Born in 1719, he became a rear-admiral at the age of 40; his greatest achievement was the defeat of the Spanish fleet off Cape St Vincent in 1780. Before that he had been Member of Parliament for Northampton, and in securing his election he is said to have spent £30,000 and thereby ruined himself. The monument to Jane, his wife, is one of the largest funerary monuments in Hampshire. A splendid piece, probably by Sir Henry Cheere, it has two seated allegorical figures. Jane Rodney died at the early age of 27 in 1757. The Georgian church was Gothicized in 1862 with the usual lamentable results. In the churchyard there is a modern sundial with a brass plate explaining, for the benefit of non-astronomers, the mystery of solar time.

The village has a triangular green and a pleasant mixture of modern, Victorian and older houses. Old Alresford Cottage near the church is a large and attractive house of about 1752. The Mothers Union was founded at Old Alresford by Mary Sumner in 1876.

Old Basing

➤ Three traumatic but quite different events have disturbed the peace of Old Basing in the last 350 years. The first of these, the siege of Basing House by Parliamentary troops in the Civil War, is too well known to recount here. Some residents of Old Basing have perpetuated the memory of the siege in their house names. Examples are Cannon Cottage (Crown Lane), Siege Cottage (The Street), and Cavalier Cottage and Round-head Cottage (Milkingpen Lane). The last two face each other across the street – one hopes that they are on friendly terms!

The second event was the construction of the Basingstoke Canal in 1788–94. It formed a loop round the earthworks of Basing House and one of its narrow bridges survives in Redbridge Lane. Traces of the canal can be seen elsewhere; there was a wharf in Crown Lane. An old story relates that one day during the construction of the canal five of the navvies disappeared – and turned up seven years later very rich men. They had apparently discovered a fortune in gold and jewellery when digging the canal bed – treasure hidden during the siege. There was once a Dead Men's Lane supposedly named after them. The local 'Legend of the Golden Calves' says that all the gold in the Marquess of Winchester's possession was transformed into little golden calves and hidden, and still awaits discovery. The only treasure ever found was in 1780, when a local watchmaker discovered 800 golden guineas.

The third event, the consequences of which will remain forever with the village, and from which the residents derive no benefit as there is no station, was the building of the

London to Southampton railway through the middle of the village on an enormous embankment. To a visitor the constant noise of trains seems intolerable but no doubt the villagers have grown accustomed to it.

The old part of Old Basing is separated from the new part by Milkingpen Lane. It would be interesting to know the origin of the name Milkingpen, and also of Swing-Swang Lane at the Redbridge Lane end of the village.

The picturesque Barton's Mill (now The Millstone Pub) on the river Loddon is a favourite with photographers (and drinkers!). You have to pass it when walking from the village car park to Basing House. You will also pass the medieval tithe barn, one of the best preserved in England.

The Street is the best of Old Basing's thoroughfares; it has several interesting old houses. No. 45 was formerly The Cricketers Arms and has the date 1593 on a chimney facing the road.

The Paulet tombs in St Mary's church are well known, but take a look at the brass plate commemorating the members of that family who are buried in the vault. Some of the dates are given alternative years, eg February 1730/1. The reason for this is that England was slow to adopt the Gregorian calendar, in which the year commenced on 1st January instead of 25th March. So between 1582 and 1752 it was the practice to give two consecutive years for dates between 1st January and 24th March, the first year for the English calendar and the second year for the European calendar.

Overton

➤ Overton was one of Bishop de Lucy's 'planned' towns of the early 13th century and its rectangular street layout is still obvious. It was mentioned as a borough in 1217–18 but it lost its urban status at some time in its history. The original village must have been north of the river near the parish church, as with Old Alresford and New Alresford.

The medieval market square was at the north end of what is now Winchester Street, and this is where the annual fair was held on 18th July. Overton was famous for its sheep fair, and before the First World War 18,000 sheep were penned in the village on that day (and still left room for thousands of visitors).

Winchester Street is a picturesque street, the houses predominantly 18th century and many of them thatched. Note the early timber-framed construction of The Greyhound inn. At the top of the hill the name Pound Road indicates the site of the old village cattle pound.

The White Hart Hotel in the centre of the village was once a popular resting-place on the London to Exeter coach road (and drinking-place on the day of the annual fair, when it stayed open all day).

Town Mill on the river Test was rebuilt in 1900 and used until the 1920s for rag-sorting and processing. A stone in the wall states that the mill was 'Recorded in the Domesday Survey 1085'. One would think that this error would have been corrected by now. William the Conqueror outlined his plans in December 1085; the Domesday survey was started and completed in 1086.

Further upstream is Quidhampton Mill, a small brick-and-flint building attached to the picturesque old mill house, only a mile or so from the source of the river Test, which is just west of Ashe church. On the Ordnance Survey map of 1817 the source is shown three-quarters of a mile further east, in Ashe Park south of the main road, indicating perhaps a fall in the underground water-table.

Paper-making for Bank of England notes, at Overton Mill in Quidhampton (what an appropriate name!), is the main occupation today (see Laverstoke), but in the early 19th century it was silk-making, most of the women in Overton then being employed in silk mills.

Pamber

➤ Ancient oak woodlands are rapidly disappearing from the countryside, so the preservation of Pamber Forest in 1980 as a nature reserve open to the public was very welcome. Owned by the Benyon Trust and covering 478 acres, it is noted for its rare insects and flowers. Rare butterflies that can be seen include the Purple Emperor and the White Admiral, and rare plants include Solomon's seal, orpine, early purple orchid and butterfly orchid. The introduction of coppices helps the growth of anemones, primroses and violets by letting in more light for a few years at a time. The quaintly-named Honeymill brook flows through the forest.

The Queens College Arms inn at Pamber End is a reminder that the College owns Pamber Priory; the inn sign showing the arms of the college is contained within a wrought-iron frame. Court Corner, north of the inn, was the meeting-place of Pamber Court in the 17th century.

Petersfield

In Petersfield there are buildings of all dates from the 16th century to the present day, but the best are of the Georgian period. Examples of older houses can be seen in Sheep Street and The Spain, and also in High Street (No. 20 'Old White Hart Ca.1590' and Nos. 17–19 dated 1613).

The Spain, the most attractive part of the town, is said to have been the centre for Spanish traders. The house named Goodyers was the home of John Goodyer (1592–1664), a noted botanist of his day, who was born at Alton and buried at Buriton. In Swan Street is the old poorhouse, given to the town by John and William Jolliffe in 1771. It was superseded by the Union workhouse in Love Lane, now the Health Centre.

The headstones in St Peter's churchyard have all been placed upright in neat rows, with the exception of one that stands by itself. This is in memory of John Small (1737–1826), one of the Hambledon cricketers. His epitaph reads:

PRAISES ON TOMBS ARE TRIFLES VAINLY SPENT
A MAN'S GOOD NAME IS HIS OWN MONUMENT

Small seems to have been one of the founders of the famous Hambledon Club, and was certainly the last survivor of its early players. His last recorded match was for Hampshire against MCC in 1798 at the age of 61. He was a member of Petersfield church choir for 75 years.

Portchester

In the whole of Hampshire there is surely no greater contrast in the two parts of a village than at Portchester. Old Portchester is hidden away at the south end of Castle Street, whereas new Portchester is a large dormitory area for Fareham and Portsmouth. Portchester was a borough in the Middle Ages, owned by Titchfield Abbey, and lay outside the castle gate, depending for its prosperity on the castle and its owners. Eventually the town declined in competition with Fareham and Portsmouth and became a quiet backwater, as the old part still is.

In old Portchester the houses are mostly of 18th-century date, with a few older ones. They vary in size, scale, texture, colour and alignment, so that though no single house is outstanding Castle Street as a whole is full of surprises – and unspoilt. Houses to note include No. 129, a former Quaker meeting-house, No. 169 (St Vincent House), once owned by Captain Cook, one of Nelson's officers, No. 172 (Dovercot), with a British Fire Office fire mark, No. 173 (Thatched Cottage – c. 1450), No. 200 (The Old Bakehouse), No. 202 (Duckett House), formerly The King's Arms, No. 211 (c.1705), formerly the Old Castle Bakery, and The Cormorant public house, the sole survivor of several inns in the old village.

The only building of any interest in new Portchester is the railway station, built in 1848 of flint and brick, with its original canopy supported on iron brackets.

St Mary's church, inside the Roman fort, has an ornate hatchment commemorating the payment of money by Queen Anne in 1710 towards the restoration of the church, and the Royal Arms of Elizabeth I dated 1577, the earliest Royal Arms in Hampshire. In the early 17th century busts began to replace effigies on monuments and memorials, and the earliest bust in Hampshire is here, on the memorial to Sir Thomas Cornwallis (1618).

Priors Dean

➤ One of the most isolated public houses in Hampshire stands high up on the plateau between Colemore and Steep, at the end of a rough track off one of the minor roads that cross this lonely countryside. No signboard announces its presence; not until you enter one of its two cosy bars can you be sure that it is a public house.

The White Horse inn, a favourite haunt of Edward Thomas, inspired his first (and longest) poem *Up in the Wind* (1914), which was adapted from a piece of prose entitled *The White Horse*. He described the isolation of this lonely inn where 'two roads cross, and not a house in sight', the occasional visitors, the wind in the trees, the calves wading in the pond, and how the signboard was stolen and thrown in the pond. To preserve the memory of the poem the signboard has not been replaced, a touching tribute to the author.

A road once passed close to the White Horse, and an important one at that, from Sussex to the Midlands via Petersfield and Alton. The lounge bar was then a smithy, so that the inn provided refreshment for the traveller and also repairs for his horse. A plaque in the bar commemorates the centenary of the birth of Edward Thomas.

Quarley

➤ St Michael's church is unique in Hampshire in having its bells outside under a cedar-shingled frame, though they are in fact rung from inside the church. There are only one or two other similar arrangements in England. One of the bells is of the 13th century, a second is dated 1636 and the third was cast in 1686 and recast in 1905. They were once rung from outside the church by young boys (for 24 shillings a year).

The other curiosity of the church is the Venetian east window, a very early example of the use of the Palladian style of architecture in England. As the inscription below it records,

Church bells at Quarley

the window was inserted by William Benson (of Wilbury House in Wiltshire) and Henry Hoare (of Stourhead), both of whom lived in Palladian-style mansions. Why they should have wished to reproduce that style in this remote Hampshire church is a mystery. (Henry Hoare junior was lord of the manor of Quarley.) The rest of the church is mainly early Norman, with some Saxon features.

Ringwood

Ringwood was mentioned in Domesday Book (Rincvede) and its market dates back to 1226 when Henry III granted a charter. It is a busy little town on market days, but not much of its ancient history is to be seen now.

The Original White Hart inn, which is on the north side of the Market Place, claims to be the first-ever White Hart inn, as its name implies. Its claim rests on an account by Sir Halliday Wagstaffe, Keeper of the Woods and Forests under Henry VII, of what happened one day in the New Forest. King Henry went hunting with his court and selected a white stag named Albert (!) for the day's sport. Albert was finally cornered near Ringwood but the ladies in the party persuaded the King not to kill him. A gold collar was put around his neck, and the name of the inn where the King dined that night was changed to The White Hart.

In fact the story of a white hart with a gold collar dates back to Pliny, who wrote that Alexander the Great did the very same thing to a stag, as also did the Emperor Charlemagne. In any case there was a White Hart inn in Southwark in 1406, long before the time of Henry VII; Shakespeare refers to it in his *Henry VI*. The Ringwood White Hart may be the earliest of that name in Hampshire but that is about all it can claim.

Monmouth House in West Street derives its name from the Duke of Monmouth, who was supposedly held prisoner there after the Battle of Sedgemoor, but the house has been rebuilt since then. Next door to it the thatched Old Cottage Restaurant may well be the oldest building in Ringwood. The lamp standard in the square commemorates Queen Victoria's Jubilee in 1887, its five ornate lanterns were restored to their rightful place a few years ago.

Other interesting buildings in Ringwood include The Meeting House, built in 1727 as a Unitarian chapel and now looking oddly out of place in its modern surroundings, and the Ringwood Almshouses of 1843, with their elaborate Tudor-style chimneys, in the street with the strange name of Quomp.

Rockbourne

Rockbourne is certainly among the half-dozen prettiest villages in Hampshire. Its old cottages and houses line the village street with the little 'stream of the rooks' (alas now often dry) running alongside; its medieval church stands adjacent to and looking down on the old manor house.

In St Andrew's church are memorials to two soldiers of the same name. Lieutenant-General Sir Eyre Coote (1726–83), when a young officer, persuaded Robert Clive to fight an immediate battle at Plassey rather than wait; fortunately for Coote's career the battle ended in victory for the British. He was from all accounts a soldier of great courage and ability, achieving many victories in India. His nephew, General Eyre Coote (1762–1823), was also a distinguished soldier, at least until bad health affected his brain and made him so eccentric that he was dismissed from the Army.

The memorial to the Reverend Thomas Durnford, minister for 42 years, records that he had seven sons and seven daughters. The odds against having seven of each sex out of fourteen children are not so great as one might think (about 4 to 1). The odds against having fourteen sons (or daughters) are 16,383 to 1.

Romsey

➤ Romsey has a long history as a borough; it received its charter of incorporation in 1607. It has had five town halls since then, including the guild-hall (now The Tudor Rose in the Corn Market) built about 1475. The town hall of 1612 (now occupied by Farmers) stands at the junction of the Market Place and The Hundred. The Audit House, which stood in the centre of the Market Place, and the old malt kiln near the west side of the abbey, used as the town hall from 1820 to 1865, have been destroyed. The present town hall is on the corner of Bell Street and the Market Place.

The main streets of Romsey – Bell Street, Middlebridge Street, Church Street and The Hundred – are very narrow; how fortunate that a bypass was built as long ago as the 1930s, otherwise many of its attractive old buildings might have been demolished in the name of progress.

A plaque in Bell Street reads: 'Body of King William Rufus carried through here on way to Winchester for burial'. It is said that William Purkess (or Purkis) brought the King's body to Winchester from the New Forest in his cart after the King's unfortunate 'accident', presumably by the easiest route, which could well have been through Romsey. 'Probably carried through here' would perhaps be more accurate.

One of Romsey's many streams, the Fishlake or Town stream, runs alongside Middlebridge Street to join the river Test. No. 48 in this street was once a mill, then a cloth warehouse, and in the 1920s became the Elite Picture Palace. The Fishlake emerges from a culvert on the west side of the bus station; the iron railings here came from the St Barbe memorial in Romsey Abbey. (There is a curious anagram on the memorial itself.)

The Romsey Working Mens Conservative Club in the Market Place stands on the site of the Swan Inn, which was one of the oldest inns in the town. A notice states that in 1642 two of Cromwell's soldiers were hanged from the wrought-iron bracket on the wall, and that the bracket is a good example of local wrought-ironwork of those days.

King John's House in Church Street is a hall-house of about 1250, one of the few in England of such an early date to have survived almost intact. In a house on the site of No. 30 Church Street Sir William Petty (1623–87) was born. A plaque describes him as an anatomist, economist, cartographer, designer and founder-member of The Royal Society. Of these occupations his chief claim to fame was as a political economist. Samuel Pepys in his *Diary* described Petty as 'one of the most rational men that ever I heard speak with a tongue, having all his notions the most distinct and clear'. His tomb is in Romsey Abbey.

In the street named The Abbey there is a mysterious carved head under an ogee arch on the wall of No. 13; this house is believed to be part of the 13th-century abbey refectory. The Bartlett Almshouses (1807) in The Meads were erected there in 1931; they formerly stood in Middlebridge Street.

At the end of The Meads, in the War Memorial Park, is a 150mm Japanese gun captured by the 14th Army in Burma in 1945 and presented to Romsey by its High Steward, Lord Louis Mountbatten, when he became the first Freeman of the borough in 1946. His home was at Broadlands just outside the town.

On the other side of the town, in Winchester road, is the former Plaza cinema, which stands on the site of the Andover Canal wharf. A public footpath follows the canal all the way from here to Timsbury, the longest water-filled stretch of the canal still surviving. An old railway signal-box that has been re-erected near a school can be seen on the right just before the first railway bridge.

Romsey has two 'twins', Paimpol on the north coast of Brittany, once an important fishing port and now a popular tourist centre, and (of course) Battenberg, a small place in Germany from whence came the royal family of that name (later the Mountbattens).

Ropley

➤ The ancient Pilgrims' Way from Winchester to Canterbury passed through Ropley. Hilaire Belloc described it in his book *The Old Road*, and his route looks convincing enough on the map, passing through Bishops Sutton, leaving the modern A31 at The Chequers and joining the minor road to Four Marks further on. The road may have been in use until the 18th century and the itinerant button-seller commemorated in St Peter's church may have used it. His memorial reads: 'Mr Wm. ROUGHCLIFF late of Sherbourn in COM:DORSET Button Seller dy'd suddainly in this Parish in his journey homeward March the 4th AD 1719/20'. (For the two dates see Basing.)

In Lyeway Lane is Archbishops Cottage, a picturesque thatched house named after William Howley (1766–1848), Archbishop of Canterbury. His father was rector of Ropley and he was born presumably at the rectory; he was fostered it is said by a woman who lived at this cottage. He became Bishop of London in 1813 and Archbishop of Canterbury in 1828, and to him fell the duty of crowning King William IV and Queen Victoria. Though Howley attained a high rank in life, Lord Grey said he was 'a poor, miserable creature', and Charles Greville described him as 'a very ordinary man'.

In Church Street is the Coffee and Reading Room, built as a men's recreation room and meeting-place in 1883 by Marianna Hagen, author of *Annals of Old Ropley* (1929).

Rowlands Castle

➤ The village name refers to the medieval castle, the remains of which, on private land south of the village centre, were cut through by the railway in 1858.

In Manor Lodge Road there is a stone memorial with the inscription: 'Here on 22 May 1944 His Majesty King George VI reviewed and bade God speed to his troops about to embark for the invasion and liberation of Europe   Deo Gratias'. For many weeks before the invasion the village was full of Army vehicles and the village green was the park for tanks. The memorial stone was placed there privately and was recently saved by the villagers when threatened by development.

St Hubert's chapel at Idsworth stands alone in a field, two miles north of Rowland's Castle. It escaped Victorian restoration because it was then disused, and in 1912 the interior was so sensitively and masterfully restored by Goodhart-Rendel that all the fittings appear to be genuinely medieval or Georgian, as indeed many of them are. The wall-paintings, dated to about 1330, are among the most important in Hampshire. The date on the notice-board ('1053 AD') presumably refers not to the present building, no part of which is earlier than Norman, but perhaps to the date of consecration of the original church (which was dedicated to St Peter and St Paul).

St Mary Bourne

People used to say that St Mary Bourne was so healthy that people born there would live for as long as they wished. Be that as it may, it seems as beautiful a place as any in which to live to a ripe old age.

The village lies in the valley of the delightfully-named Bourne rivulet, which rises at Hurstbourne Tarrant, trickles through St Mary Bourne and meets the Test beyond Hurstbourne Priors. At least in a normal year it trickles; it has been known to flood the main street after heavy rain.

A narrow bridge in the centre of the village crosses the stream where it swings from one side of the main street to the other. Near the bridge there is a cast iron lamp post, the only survivor from the days when the street lamps used oil. It was erected in 1897 to commemorate the Diamond Jubilee of Queen Victoria.

On both sides of the main street there are attractive old cottages, some thatched and timber-framed, such as The Old Plough, formerly an inn, with its long low thatched roof, and Hillview Cottages, perhaps the oldest in the village, with a Sun Assurance fire mark on the wall. Quite a contrast are the

Holdway Almshouses, built in 1862 in flint and brick in a rather half-hearted attempt at Gothic.

The most important object in St Peter's church is the Norman Tournai marble font, the largest of the four of this type in Hampshire. Of the original font only the bowl survives; note the carvings of doves drinking out of cups, symbolising the Holy Communion – this is rare in Norman decoration.

In the south chapel there is a cross-legged effigy of Sir Roger des Andelys, who fought in the Crusade against the Albigenses (French heretics) in 1209–17; it was made about 1300, some time after his death. Cross-legged effigies first appeared about 1250 and remained in fashion until about 1350.

From 1380 to 1561 all 16 rectors except one were knights. They were probably absentee rectors who employed a curate to look after the church services for them (see Hurstbourne Priors). A curious gravestone in the churchyard reads: 'The terrestrial part of Robert Longman lys here sleeping 1708'.

The annual fair held until about 1830 in the Summerhaugh, the open space in the centre of the village, was known as the Bourne Revel, and from what is known of the festivities a name richly deserved. The cudgel-fights, on a stage opposite the Plough inn, were the main attraction; young men known as 'back-sworders' struck each other on the head until they drew an inch of blood. Other strange activities included 'jingling' matches, in which the 'jingler' (a person with a bell in each hand) had to be caught by his blindfolded opponents, and yawning matches (!) for prizes of Cheddar cheeses.

Selborne

The small open space in front of St Mary's church is known as The Plestor. The name is derived from 'playstow', which in the Middle Ages was a playground. Gilbert White described The Plestor as a square piece of ground in which once stood a vast oak tree, blown down in the storm of 1703. The oak was surrounded by steps and seats and the square was a favourite resort of young and old on summer evenings.

Gilbert White's gravestone in the churchyard has simply the

initials 'G.W.' and the date of his death. Also there is the grave of 'The Trumpeter', by name John Newland, who was the leader of the local agricultural workers' riots in 1830; he summoned his supporters by means of a trumpet. After the riots he took refuge in the woods around Selborne and escaped arrest. The mob attacked the poorhouses at Selborne and Headley, and so frightened the vicar of Selborne that he reduced his tithes on the spot from £600 to £300 a year. The Selborne poorhouse (Fisher's Buildings) is in Gracious Street.

Facing The Wakes, Gilbert White's home, is a small building that was once a butcher's shop. In his *Garden Kalendar* White records that in 1756 he planted four lime trees in front of it to hide 'the sight of blood and filth from ye windows' (see plaque). Only two of the trees survive.

At the far south end of the village there is a unique drinking-fountain, a splendid piece of Victorian ironwork, in the form of a fierce lion's head, flanked by windmills, the water flowing from the lion's mouth into a trough. It is inscribed 'Presented by' but there is no name. The adjacent door has an inscription: 'This water supply was given to Selborne by voluntary subscriptions in memory of Gilbert White 1894'. Behind the door there is a hydraulic ram that pumped water to stand-pipes in the village until 1934, when piped water was supplied.

Sherborne St John

Few churches in Hampshire have as many curious and interesting things as St Andrew's. On the ancient brick porch (dated 1533) note the name of the donor on the outside – James Spyre, and again on the inner doorway – Jamys Spier. They were not too fussy about their spelling in those days.

The inscription on the memorial to George Beverly on the south wall of the nave reads: 'Erected in the 29th yeare of King Charles ye 2nd AD 1678'. Obviously put up by a faithful royalist, it dates the reign of Charles II from 1649, the year of Charles I's execution. On the pulpit we find the maker's autograph carved on the front: 'Mad by Henri Sly 1634'. Spelling was still not a craftsman's strong point.

The Brocas chapel contains the imposing tomb of Ralph Pexall and his wife (c.1535) and several old brasses of the Brocas family, the one dated 1360 being the oldest in Hampshire. The early 16th-century Dutch stained glass in the chapel window, depicting various scenes on the theme of 'public humiliation', is the best of its type and date in the county.

The gravestone of George Hickson (nearest the church east of the porch) reads: 'He had lived above 20 years in the service of William Chute Esq. as whipper in and huntsman and continued after he died in the family as coachman. Respected while living and lamented when dead'. Was he the original ghostly coachman? But wait, that is not the end of it. There is a local legend of a ghostly carriage that used to drive up to the front door of Wyeford Farm, three miles away, and then disappear. But unfortunately for this story Wyeford Farm was not the home of William Chute or of George Hickson. Nevertheless . . . !

The middle cottage of a row of cottages on the main road (Nos. 2–6 Aldermaston Road) once looked exactly the same as its neighbours (it has a porch and a notice-board now). It was built as a chapel of the Plymouth Brethren and had to be disguised or concealed from the disapproving eyes of the established Church. The Reverend J. N. Darby founded the Plymouth Brethren, an austere Protestant sect, in 1830. It enforces strict standards of behaviour and forbids its members to take up certain trades and professions.

The village pond nearby, screened from passing traffic by trees, is the source of the Wey brook. The Ordnance Survey describes it as a watercress bed!

Silchester

➤ The site of the Roman town of Calleva Atrebatum is too well known to enlarge upon here, but a visit to the not-so-well-known Calleva Museum, on the east side of the common, is recommended; it is open during daylight hours. The earliest description of the site of the Roman town was by John Leland, the king's antiquary, in about 1540.

Silchester Common, larger than nearby Tadley Common, is a useful open space for the villagers. The by-laws forbid bows, crossbows and catapults, and also fishing, shooting and hunting. Fishing might be possible in the tiny streams on the common, and shooting at rabbits, but hunting – for what?

At the north-west corner of the common, on the county boundary, stands the Imp Stone. It may be a Roman milestone on which the word 'Imperator' was once visible; a local legend says that it was thrown from Roman Silchester by a giant.

Going clockwise round the common from the Imp Stone are the Ebenezer Primitive Cottage of 1864, the Calleva Museum and the war memorial, which records that most unusually more men of the village died in the Second World War (six) than in the First World War (five).

Near the Calleva Arms public house is Silchester House with its remarkable clock-tower, where painted clock-jacks can be seen striking the hours. Dial House on the corner has an old sundial and a brass plate informing us that a dial post was first erected here in 1716 and renewed in 1815 and again in 1871.

There are many interesting things in St Mary's church, which is situated just within the Roman town wall. Its plan is unusual – a long chancel and a short nave with aisles. Roman bricks are visible in its walls and buttresses. The organ is thought to date from about 1770 and is quite rare. A charity board states that Richard Hyde gave to twelve poor inhabitants the rent and profits of a house and two piddles of land known by the name of Flexditch. A piddle, or more correctly a pightle, was a small field or enclosure. There were six rectors in 1349, a reminder of the terrible consequences of the Black Death. The predecessor of this church is the earliest known Christian church in Great Britain; it lies under the soil in the Roman town.

Soberton

➤ The odd feature in Soberton church is the processional path through the old part of the tower, which was retained when the tower was extended. The passage was originally made because there was no room outside the west end of the

Medieval carving at Soberton church

church for processions, which were an important part of the church ritual in medieval times.

High up on the outside of the tower is a medieval carving of a skull between two heads with a key and a bucket or purse. This carving has given rise to the legend that the tower was built by a butler and a dairymaid. (It would have taken them a long time, in their spare time!) The legend was perpetuated by a stone, set in the tower when it was restored, that reads: THIS TOWER ORIGINALLY BUILT BY SERVANTS WAS RESTORED BY SERVANTS 1881.

On the strength of the legend a total of £70 was subscribed for the restoration by domestic staff all over Hampshire. Another inscription inside the tower records their contribution and refers to the old tradition.

West Walk, south of the village, is a small remnant of the Forest of Bere, which once stretched from Romsey to the Sussex boundary and was seven miles wide. The first people known to have made use of the forest were the Romans; remains of their ironworks were discovered when one of the car parks was made. In Saxon and medieval times the forest was used for hunting and to provide wood for building; it has

151

now been mostly taken over for agriculture. Some old oaks remain here and there, however, and new oaks and conifers have been planted. There are three trails to follow from the various car parks; in spring when the bluebells are out is a good time to visit this not-so-well-known woodland.

A plaque on the pillar-box at Droxford old railway station records that in a special train here Winston Churchill and his staff spent some days making crucial decisions immediately prior to the invasion of Europe in 1944. His 'staff' included Commonwealth Prime Ministers and Allied military leaders.

Sopley

A notice in the porch apologising for the 'unsocial behaviour of the resident bats' provides a strange welcome to the ancient church of St Michael and All Angels, which stands on a hillock above the river Avon not far from the county boundary. One of the medieval carvings in the church is of a man's face with his tongue sticking out – more unsocial behaviour!

Two of the Willis family memorials deserve special mention: James Willis, who was the vicar from 1779 to 1835, and General Sir George Willis, who was awarded twelve decorations by various countries.

Sopley has one of the shortest one-way road systems in Hampshire – each of the streets being no more than 250 yards long. It must be the smallest village in the county with a one-way system. Sopley Forge is a working blacksmith's; the building is about 100 years old and there was a blacksmith in Sopley in the late 19th century. The house opposite was formerly The Smith's Arms – the name though painted over is still legible.

South Hayling

An attempt in the 1820s to develop South Hayling as a seaside resort proved a failure; a hotel and a partly-completed crescent of houses was the result. A few large Edwardian villas were built later but nothing much happened until the 1930s when development began in earnest.

Norfolk Crescent was begun in 1825 and never completed. A grandiose terrace like those in London and Bath, though admirable in conception, it was out of place on this wind-swept shore. The Royal Hotel was built in 1826 and later enlarged. The neighbouring inn, The Royal Shades, was built as an adjunct to the hotel; though its signboard reads 'A coaching inn c.1800', there were no regular coaches until the bridge was built in 1824.

Further east on the sea front is Seacourt House, which is interesting on two counts. Hayling Island was once infested with mosquitoes; in 1921 at this house John Marshall inaugurated the Hayling Mosquito Control, the first anti-mosquito scheme in Great Britain. In the grounds he built an eleven-room laboratory and this became the British Mosquito Control Institute; visitors came from all over the world. The happy outcome is that the salt-marsh mosquito is now rare. Marshall was also a devotee of real tennis. At Seacourt House in 1910–11 he built the last full-size real tennis court in Europe; the World Open Real Tennis Tournament has been held there. Real tennis (more correctly court or royal tennis) was brought to Europe by the Crusaders and proved most popular in France, especially in monasteries; it later became popular with royalty. It became established in England in the 14th century and was mentioned by Chaucer. The more popular lawn tennis was not patented until 1874.

At the east end of the sea front, on the shore, is the old lifeboat house, a brick building with a slate roof. Opposite is a row of former coastguard cottages and a peculiar octagonal building known as The Round House (in the grounds of the Suntrap School), which used to house an X-ray machine.

The famous journalist and social reformer W. T. Stead lived at No 30 Selsmore Road from 1895 to 1912 (see plaque). He was editor of the *Pall Mall Gazette* and founder of the *Review of Reviews*. It was said that in the late 19th century nobody had exercised a greater influence on national events. A spiritualist interested in psychical research, he was drowned on the ill-fated maiden voyage of the *Titanic*; he had told friends beforehand that he would not return from it.

Southwick

➤ Not much in the old part of the village seems to have changed over the years, for in High Street and West Street there is hardly a building to be seen less than about 100 years old and most of them are much older. No single building stands out but the timber-framed cottages and 18th-century brick houses in its two main streets make an attractive whole. There is even a tiny village green with a pump, and a village smithy still flourishing. The village has retained its old character because of its long ownership by Southwick Estates.

A priory of Augustinian canons moved here from Portchester in about 1150. They were dissolved in 1538 and the property was given to John White who converted the priory into a house. Recent excavations on the site have proved that both the priory and the later mansion underwent several rebuildings. Many oyster shells were found, indicating that oysters and no doubt other shellfish were part of the monks' diet.

The church of St James (St James-Without-The-Priory-Gate to give it its full name) has the status of a 'peculiar', which means that by ancient privilege it does not come under the bishop's jurisdiction. It was rebuilt in 1566, a rare example of a post-Reformation Tudor church, for there was very little church rebuilding at that time.

That apart, the church is chiefly remarkable for its furnishings, which give it a charming unrestored atmosphere. There is a three-decker pulpit, a gallery, two family box-pews and a reredos painted to simulate marble. The old pews, alas, have been replaced by modern ones. There is a tragic memorial to the four sons of General Pakenham. One died at Lucknow, one at Fort Gwalior, one at Inkerman in the 'fatal sandbag battery' (!?), and one died 'of decline' in the Red Sea.

In 1900 there were more than 80 breweries in Hampshire, but in 1988 there were only two in production. In the 19th century a village public house often had its own brewery; as transport improved however most of the local breweries moved to the towns. The Golden Lion had its own brewery from at least 1800. Behind the inn are the brewery buildings; the entire brewing machinery is contained within one room, a rare survival from those times. Brewing ceased in 1956, when the brewer, Dick Olding, retired after 50 years there. The quality of the beer made there is remembered by the locals with nostalgic affection. The machinery has been restored to working order and the brewhouse is open by appointment.

Steep

Steep by name and steep by nature, the village lies on the lower slopes of the hangers that tower above the scattered groups of houses below. Not without good reason is this area known as 'Little Switzerland'; the wooded heights and combes of this western end of the Weald form scenery quite different from the rest of Hampshire.

Incredibly, coaches from Petersfield to Winchester and Alton once made their way up the face of Stoner Hill. This old road can still be followed as a track from the foot of the zigzag road that was constructed about 1826 to replace it.

From the top of the chalk escarpment magnificent views unfold, 'sixty miles of South Downs at one glance' as the writer and poet Edward Thomas described them. He came to Steep with his family in 1906 and at first lived at Berryfield Cottage (now simply Berryfield) at Ashford Chace, at the very foot of the hangers opposite the awesome cleft of Lutcombe.

In 1909 the Thomases moved to a new house (still named The Red House) on top of the escarpment in Cockshott Lane. This house was the subject of Thomas's poem *The New House*, which is engraved on his memorial window in All Saints church. This house eventually became too expensive to maintain and in 1913 the family moved downhill to the village, to one of the semi-detached Yew Cottages, now known as No. 2 Yew Cottage, which was the setting for his poem *Old Man*.

This house proved too small for them and Thomas got away whenever he could; ever restless, he joined the Army in 1915. His family moved to Essex in 1916. A memorial to him stands on Shoulder of Mutton Hill, a favourite spot of his, which can be reached from Cockshott Lane; it reads:

This hillside is dedicated to the memory of Edward Thomas   Poet   Born in Lambeth 3 March 1878   Killed in the Battle of Arras 9 April 1917   'and I rose up and knew that I was tired and continued my journey.'

Not far from No. 2 Yew Cottage is Hillcroft, on which is a plaque recording that T. Sturge Moore (1870–1944), the poet and wood-engraver, lived there from 1922 to 1932. The plaque has the wrong date, because he moved there in 1919.

Edward Thomas's memorial window in the church was engraved by Laurence Whistler. Two other memorials are worthy of note: Basil Marden was killed by an avalanche while climbing Mount Aconcagua in the Andes in 1928, and Martha Legg died in 1829 at the age of 105.

Lower down the village, beyond the church, is The Harrow Inn, which will prove to be a pleasant surprise to those who think that real old English country pubs have disappeared. Two small cosy low-beamed bars with huge log fires, beer straight from the barrel, home-made soup and crusty bread and an absence of fruit machines create an atmosphere rarely found today.

The Council planners want to make the countryside around Steep into an organised recreational area 'suitable for tourists to be channelled through', to use their phraseology. The locals are naturally against this, and so too would be Edward Thomas, who if he knew what was afoot would be turning in his grave. The environment of Steep should remain as natural as it was in his day.

Steventon

➤ The Reverend George Austen, rector of Steventon for over 40 years, had eight children all of whom except one lived to a good age. Such being the irony of life, that one had more to give to the world than any of them. She was of course Jane Austen, one of the great English novelists.

She was born in 1775 in the old rectory, the site of which is marked by an old pump enclosed within railings, in the field at the corner of the lane that leads to the church. The house was pulled down in 1826; the pump would probably have been outside the kitchen.

Jane lived here for 25 years, and on most Sundays walked up the lane to the church to listen to her father's sermon (with what enthusiasm we do not know). The lane, then known as Church Walk, is barely wide enough for two cars to pass; at the end is the church and the former Steventon Manor of 1876, which has recently been rebuilt after lying derelict since the war. The medieval village was near the church, and traces of it may have been more obvious in Jane Austen's day than now.

The rectory stood at the very east end of the village and on its east side was flanked by one of the thatched mud walls that were once common in the county. Jane Austen would probably not recognise the village of Steventon now, certainly not the massive railway viaduct. The countryside here, if not exceptionally beautiful, has always been quiet and pleasant, and we can appreciate Jane's depression at the thought of leaving here for the noise and unfamiliarity of Bath.

St Nicholas's church was old even when Jane worshipped there, for it dates from the 13th century. There is a mass-dial or sundial on the right-hand side of the entrance. This means that the doorway has been reset there from the south side of the church, for a sundial would have been useless on a west-facing wall. The tower is flanked by bays that seem to serve no purpose, for there are no aisles to which they could have been extensions.

The memorials are all to the Austens and the Digweeds, who lived in the manor house. The graves of Jane's brother James, who succeeded his father as rector in 1801, and of her nephew William Knight, who was rector for 50 years, are in the churchyard. The tragic memorial to the latter's three daughters, aged five, four and three, records that they all died of scarlet fever in the same year.

Stockbridge

Stockbridge is sited where the valley of the river Test is crossed by a causeway, at the junction of two routes, one from Winchester to Salisbury and the other from Andover to Southampton. On the east and west the roads climb steeply out of the village. At least six streams flow under High Street and the causeway.

The bridge of 1799 over the Test was rebuilt in 1963 to cope with modern traffic. The 15th-century bridge was crossed by John Leland in his travels, and the inscription that was on it is recorded on the present bridge: 'Say of your cheryte a paternoster and a ave for the sowllys of John Gylmyn otherwyse seyd Lokke and Richard Gater and Margarete the wyf of the forsayd John and Richard fownderys and makerys of the sayd brydge yn whos sowllys God have mercy'.

The White Hart Inn, if perhaps not the most imposing, is certainly the most picturesque building in Stockbridge, with its upper storey supported on cast-iron Tuscan columns. The strange grooves on the top of the old churchyard wall, which abuts on to the inn, are said to have been made by the constant sharpening of sword-blades.

The most imposing building is The Grosvenor Hotel, classical and also with Tuscan columns, which incorporates the old Market Room. Stockbridge first had a market in 1190; its fair, mainly for sheep, lasted from 1221 to 1932.

Stockbridge is probably most famous for having been a 'rotten' borough, because in spite of its small size it sent two Members to Parliament from 1563 to 1832. The elections in Stockbridge were also accompanied by prime examples of the bribery and corruption that attended English elections before the Reform Acts. By 1790 votes were being openly sold for £70 each, which was equivalent to 140 weeks' wages for a labourer. Nowadays votes are bought by more subtle methods.

In 1790 one of the two ringleaders of the election bribery was John Bucket (or Buckett), one of the local inn keepers. He is buried in the old churchyard, and his epitaph reads:

In Memory of John Buckett, many years landlord of
the King's Head Inn in this Borough who departed
this life November 25th 1802 aged 67 years.
And is alas poor BUCKET gone?
Farewell convivial honest JOHN.
Oft at the well by fatal stroke
Buckets like Pitchers must be broke
In this same motley shifting scene
How various have thy fortunes been.

Twelve more lines follow, of which the last four read:

Then rise immortal Bucket rise
And claim thy station in the skies
'Twixt amphora & Pisces shine
Still guarding Stockbridge with his sign.

The chancel, all that remains of the old church, is hidden in
the trees in a corner of the churchyard. The rest of the church
was demolished in 1863; it is said that the chancel defied all
attempts at demolition.

The Common Marsh can be reached by a footpath that starts
near the Waggon & Horses inn. It was granted to the lords of
the manor by charter, and burgesses of Stockbridge may use it
for pasturing cattle – six beasts each, though this number may
be varied at the annual Court Leet. The procedures at the Court
date back some 900 years and are of great interest to historians.
The Court and the Common Marsh are now in the safe hands
of the National Trust.

Stoke Charity

➤ Few churches in Hampshire are as beautifully situated as
St Michael's, which stands in complete isolation above the little
river Dever. It is approached by a path across fields in which
once stood the manor house and probably also the medieval
village.

In the church are several 15th- and 16th-century tombs

with brass effigies of great historical interest. That of Thomas Hampton and his wife also depicts their eight children. Altogether this is the best collection of tombs and brasses of this period in Hampshire.

An even rarer treasure in the church is the Mass of St Gregory, a piece of medieval sculpture found in the wall in 1849. It was probably hidden there in about 1550 because of a Parliamentary statute decreeing that all images be destroyed. The legend of St Gregory recounts how a vision of Christ appeared at a mass to convince doubters of His existence. This is the best-preserved of the three surviving in England.

Part of the church is Norman – the north arcade with its enormous octagonal pier and the elaborate chancel arch with zigzag decoration. All in all you will not find many churches in the county more interesting than this one.

The village was named after Henry de la Charité, who owned the manor in the 13th century. William Cobbett came here in 1825 and in his *Rural Rides* cited the village as an example of the decay of parishes. He wrote that 'the parish formerly contained ten farms, and it now contains but two. . . . There used to be ten well-fed families . . . these, taking five to a family, made fifty well-fed people. And now, all are half-starved, except the curate and the two families (ie the two farm families).

Stratfield Saye

➤ The long stretch of grassy track on the county boundary, known as The Devil's Highway, is part of the Roman road from London to Silchester. From London it changed direction near Bagshot and then followed a straight course to the east gate of the Roman town.

St Mary's church in the park was built in 1758 in the form of a Greek cross and has been restored to its original Georgian appearance. The Georgians did away with the medieval church, which was nearer Stratfield Saye House; they called it 'that ugly uncouth structure'. The Victorians in their turn could hardly restrain themselves from doing likewise to this 'monster of ecclesiastical ugliness' as they called it, but somehow it survived.

As you would expect the memorials are mostly to the Dukes of Wellington. The Iron Duke himself worshipped here from 1819 to 1852. Under the trees in the churchyard is the grave of John Baylie (died 1777) whose headstone reads:

> Asleep beneath this humble Stone
> Lies honest harmless simple John
> Who free from Guilt & Care & Strife,
> Here clos'd his inoffensive Life.
> His worth was great, his failings few,
> He practis'd all the good he knew,
> And did no harm, his only sin
> Was that he lov'd a drop of Gin,
> And when his favourite was not near
> Contented, took his horn of Beer.

There is more to follow, but that is the best part of it.

Stratfield Turgis

All Saints church, empty and derelict, stands completely hidden by trees at the end of a lane off the A33. Its walls are covered in creepers and its gravestones lie higgledy-piggledy in the nettles and undergrowth, yet it was restored in 1901 and was in use up to 1970. Near the porch is the grave of John Mears (died 1872) who was for 33 years pad-groom to the first Duke of Wellington.

A footpath crosses the adjoining field to the bank of the gently-flowing river Loddon, winding its way towards Stratfield Saye Park and on to meet the Thames at Shiplake. Opposite the church is Turgis Court, a fine Georgian house surrounded by a moat; it stands on the site of Stratfield Turgis manor house.

Turgis Green is the home of Stratfield Turgis Cricket Club, which is said to have been founded in 1812. There are two public houses in Stratfield Turgis: The Cricketers at Turgis

Green and The Wellington Arms Hotel, a building in Grecian style, on the main road.

Swanmore

➤ Stephen Leacock, the humorous writer, was born in 1869 at Leacock House near the parish church. He was taken to Canada at the age of six, and eventually became a professor of economics at Montreal University. He achieved great success with his books of humorous essays and stories, titles such as *Literary Lapses* and *Nonsense Novels* becoming world-famous. His gentle humour was founded on the inconsistencies and absurdities of ordinary situations to demonstrate the comic elements in them. His weapon was not propaganda or carica-ture but satire; very few writers have used it more effectively.

Tadley

➤ In the early days of balloons it is said that one came down in Tadley and an awestruck villager, on being asked by the balloonist where he was, replied 'Tadley, God save us' (or in another version of the story 'Tadley, God help us'). The man in the balloon had never heard of Tadleygodsaveus, or even of Tadley, so he was none the wiser.

An old verse starts 'Tadley, God help us, back of beyond' and finishes 'Tadley ain't nearly as bad as you think!' Few visitors today would agree with the last statement. Tadley is too near Reading for comfort, and it has been swamped with housing estates for commuters. Its population in 1891 was 1,115; in 1981 it was 8,827 and growing rapidly. It has recently given itself a Town Council, thus becoming Hampshire's newest town.

What is left of old Tadley is hidden away on the south side of the town. In Manse Lane, Malthouse Lane and Knapp Lane there are some fine old thatched cottages, such as Cons' Cottage (1628), Pear Tree Cottage, Crooked Cottage (once a general store) and Highbury Cottage. Malthouse Lane was once the commercial centre of Tadley.

The brick-built 'Old Meeting' United Reformed church (1662) dates from 1718–19, a reminder of the days when nonconformity attracted many people. The date 1662 refers to the Act of Uniformity that ejected unordained Puritan ministers from their churches in favour of Anglican ministers. This marked the beginning of that great social and religious division between 'church' and 'chapel' that persisted almost to the present day.

That is about all there is of old Tadley except for St Peter's church, a mile by road from the town. If you persevere in finding it and obtaining the key you will be well-rewarded, for it has a charming unrestored interior with 17th-century pews and gallery and a pulpit dated 1650, a rare example of the Commonwealth period. In complete contrast is the modern church of St Paul, which has a remarkable design whereby the high-pitched roof is supported on timber frames and the walls carry no weight.

At least the town still has Tadley Common, all 100 acres of it. The rights of the local people on the common include grazing, taking gravel and stone, and cutting heath for broom-making. The great industry in Tadley once was broom-making, using birch trees from Pamber Forest; no less than 100,000 were made annually in the heyday of the industry. Broadhalfpenny Lane, on the west side of the common, may have the same derivation as Broadhalfpenny Down at Hambledon (the toll paid to the lord of the manor for a booth at the fair). The public house on the corner is The Treacle Mine, perhaps named after the legend of 'treacle mines' at Tilehurst, Reading (possibly from Old English *treag* meaning 'flint'). Several prehistoric flint implements have been found around Tilehurst. About 100 years ago many cottages in Tadley were owned by gypsies, who for once in a while gave up their wandering life and settled down here.

Thruxton

In 1823 a Roman mosaic pavement was discovered in a field between Thruxton and Fyfield. The site was then lost for over 70 years, when the pavement was rediscovered and removed to the British Museum. Strangely there were no signs of any walls or buildings at the site. There used to be a legend in Thruxton that 'golden gates' had been found there.

In the village there is an old milestone inscribed 'LXVIIII Miles from London V from Andover' (69 is usually written LXIX). It has not been there many years, having been removed from the A303, which was once the turnpike road. Milestones usually gave distances to places on either side, not to two places in the same direction.

There are many interesting and attractive old houses in the village. The older ones (eg Well Cottage) are built of chalk dug from pits on London Hill, with a thatched roof and flint foundations ('a good hat and a good pair of shoes' as the local saying has it). Flint was also used for the walls, sometimes combined with brick (eg Goose Acre); it was cheap and indestructible. Thatched roofs were common until the 19th century, when slate became more widely available with the advent of cheap transport. There were one or more thatchers living in Thruxton up to 1848, but there was no mention of a bricklayer until 1862.

The parish church is always locked; it contains some early and interesting effigies, including the earliest effigy of a knight in Hampshire (13th century) and a wooden effigy of an Elizabethan lady wearing a ruff.

Tichborne

➤ Tichborne is famous of course for the Tichborne Claimant and the resulting Victorian court case, and for the Tichborne Dole, the charity that has been dispensed since the 13th century. It is a charming little village, hidden away off the beaten track. Its oldest house is probably the Old Post Office (about 1600) opposite The Tichborne Arms.

St Andrew's church is unique in Hampshire (and apart from St Nicholas's in Arundel unique in England) in having a Roman Catholic chapel within an Anglican church, the Tichborne family having been steadfast Catholics. The chancel is Norman

St Peter's Church, Tichborne

in date but Anglo-Saxon in style; it was probably built by local Saxon craftsmen – note the double-splayed windows and pilaster strips, typical Saxon features.

The memorial to Richard Tichborne (died 1619) who 'lived one yeare six monethes & too daies' has a sad story attached to it, if we are to believe it. Legend has it that a gypsy woman, on being refused food at Tichborne House, laid a curse on young Richard, to the effect that he would drown on a certain day. When that day arrived the servants were ordered to take him up on the downs for safety, well away from the river, but when they were not looking he fell out of his carriage into a cart-rut of water and was drowned. The truth of the story can be assessed from the fact that the first baby-carriage or perambulator in England was made for the third Duke of Devonshire in 1730.

Titchfield

Titchfield had a market and toll at the time of Domesday Book (one of the only two tolls in Hampshire), and in the Middle Ages was an important market town with a relatively large population. It depended to a great extent for its prosperity on the abbey founded here in 1232, which eventually owned 15 manors with over 60 villages. In the 18th century the population of Titchfield trebled to nearly 3,000 by 1801.

Titchfield is an unlikely place in which to find the second oldest canal in England. In 1611 the Earl of Southampton blocked the mouth of the river Meon with a shingle bank and constructed a canal from the village to an outlet on the coast west of the former Meon estuary. The purpose of the canal was to carry goods to and from the mill, the tannery and the village, and also to irrigate the water-meadows on either side by means of sluice-gates. The blocking of the estuary however put paid to Titchfield's importance as a port. The first canal in England (since Roman times) was at Exeter in 1564–6.

The canal at Titchfield still exists and can be followed on foot from the village to the old sea-lock under the bridge on the coast road. The original side walls of the lock survive, made of stone taken perhaps from the old abbey buildings. Unlike modern locks this lock had only a single pair of gates, so boats had to wait for the tide before they could enter the canal.

Stone churches were uncommon in the early Anglo-Saxon period; most were built of wood and the Saxons in fact had no word for building in stone. They eventually mastered the art well enough to erect cathedrals and minster churches, but of these very little has survived above ground level. There are a few stone churches of the early period in England but most were destroyed in the Danish wars of the 9th century.

The only certain survival in Hampshire of the early Anglo-Saxon period is the lower part of the tower of St Peter's, Titchfield, which was then, as it is now, the porch. The western porch was a feature of early Anglo-Saxon churches; it was superseded in the later Saxon period by the western tower, which became a common feature of medieval churches. At Titchfield the porch was extended to form a tower in the 12th or 13th century. Roman materials re-used in the construction of the porch, such as the bonding course of tiles at a height of 14 ft, also suggest an early Saxon date for it. It is likely that the porch dates from the late 7th or early 8th century, making it the oldest piece of church architecture in Hampshire. The church of which it was a part may have been built by St Wilfrid, who was a missionary in Sussex in AD 681–6.

Artificial fishponds were introduced to England after the Norman Conquest, constructed at first by royalty and later by bishops and monasteries (see Old Alresford and Beaulieu). Fishponds were an important part of the medieval economy; they supplied fresh fish for bishops and other wealthy people and their guests. The design of fishponds remained virtually unchanged for hundreds of years. Over 80 fishpond sites have been discovered in Hampshire, a large number when it is remembered that ponds on chalk need layers of clay to retain the water. At Titchfield four large fishponds can be seen from the public footpath on the west side of the abbey.

Totton

➤ Before it became a town Totton was called 'England's largest village' because of the size of its population (23,084 in 1981). It was once described as a pretty hamlet in a picturesque and beautiful neighbourhood (Hunt's *Directory of Hampshire*, 1852). Totton is now a sad example of all that is worst in modern architecture and planning. If the name of W H Smith's superstore 'DO IT ALL' prompts you to a thorough perambulation of the streets of Totton, you will see few buildings of any merit. One curious thing is a large inscription on No. 1 Rumbridge Street: 'BATTS CORNER LONDON 77 MILES BOURNEMOUTH 24 MILES'. Batt was a shopkeeper who is said to have sold everything except food.

Totton is 'twinned' with Le Loroux Bottereau, a small place twelve miles east of Nantes. Perhaps Totton felt that it had to compensate for its own short name by 'twinning' with a place that had as long a name as possible.

Red Bridge over the Test, partly in Totton, partly in Southampton, dates from the 17th century. The bridge over the other arm of the Test was built in 1793. This river crossing has always been important, and a bridge was first recorded in 1226.

The Test Way footpath starts at the Salmon Leap public house at the end of Testwood Lane and crosses the lower Test valley on planks. There is a gradual change from salt-marsh to freshwater-marsh; the path at first crosses a large expanse of reeds and then an area where hay was once grown. Birds often seen here include wintering wildfowl and waders, reed-warblers and snipe. The water-meadows support a rich variety of plants.

Tufton

➤ The little Norman church of St Mary at Tufton is hidden away on the southern outskirts of Whitchurch. It has a simple but beautiful Early English chancel with three-bay arcading, and a Norman chancel arch.

On the north wall opposite the south doorway is a medieval wall-painting of St Christopher. He was depicted more often than any other saint and probably few churches in those days were without a picture of him.

St Christopher paintings are always opposite the south door because it was a convenient place for travellers and passers-by to see them; St Christopher gave special protection against sudden death, a comforting reassurance to travellers in the Middle Ages.

These wall-paintings were done by mixing the pigments with boiling water and applying them to slightly damp plaster made of lime; the paint then dried into the plaster. In those days only colours made from the grinding of rocks or clays could be used. The artist was not allowed to make a realistic painting because of the Commandment that forbids the making of graven images.

Twyford

Twyford means 'double ford' and the river Itchen has always been an important adjunct to the village, for at the time of Domesday Book there were six mills here. The Bishop of Winchester was then the lord of the manor.

The church bells are inevitably associated with the story of William Davies. It is said that he lost his way in a fog on his way home and heard the Twyford bells just in time to avoid falling into a chalk-pit. In gratitude for his escape he bequeathed in 1754 £1 every year to the ringers on condition that the bells be rung twice on 7th October. This custom is still continued and is followed by the Ringers' Dinner at which Davies's will is read out.

An even noisier celebration survived in Twyford until 1880. On 26th November (St Clement's Day) the 'Clem Supper' was held at The Bugle Inn. The toast to 'the blacksmiths' was followed by the firing of an anvil with gunpowder. St Clement is the patron saint of blacksmiths, but why Twyford should have been so enthusiastic about him is a mystery.

St Mary's church, rebuilt in 1876–7 in Perpendicular style, has two memorials by famous sculptors. The one to Georgiana Naylor by Flaxman has an extraordinarily effusive inscription making her out to be an absolute paragon of virtue. The memorial to her father Bishop Shipley by Nollekens is more restrained.

In the church is a copy of the Elizabethan seating plan, which allotted people their place according to their status. The yew tree, at least 650 years old, is thought to be the oldest clipped yew in the country.

Houses of note in the village include The Old Rectory and Mildmay House (five bays, about 1700), both near the church, Twyford House (seven bays, Queen Anne) where Bishop Shipley entertained Benjamin Franklin, and Twyford School, alluded to by Thomas Hughes in unflattering terms in *Tom Brown's Schooldays*.

The Lower St Cross, Mill Lane and Park Gate Turnpike was authorized in 1810, exactly 100 years after the first Hampshire turnpike, and two toll-houses survive at Twyford, one north of and one south of the village, though both have been somewhat altered.

Upper Clatford

➤ The name Clatford has an unusual meaning – 'ford where burdock grew'. (Burdock is the plant that produces the sticky burs that people love to throw on one another.) The village is situated at the junction of the river Anton and its tributary the Pillhill brook and is overlooked by the hill-fort on Bury Hill, an Iron Age stronghold abandoned about AD 100.

In 1813 Robert Tasker (see Abbotts Ann) removed his Abbotts Ann Foundry to Upper Clatford; it was later renamed Waterloo Ironworks and became famous for every kind of cast-iron and wrought-iron implements and farm machinery. The history of Taskers is displayed at Andover Museum. Their first traction-engine was completed in 1869 and was driven to the Royal Agricultural Show at Southampton, the first steam-engine ever to travel along these quiet country roads.

Of the ironworks nothing now remains; modern houses cover the entire site, but on the opposite side of the road there are two reminders of those days. The Waterloo Workmens Hall (1867), now the Waterloo Free church, was used by the employees for evening recreation, and the 14 houses forming Waterloo Terrace were built for some of the foundry workers.

There are many attractive 18th-century and 19th-century houses in Upper Clatford and its neighbour Goodworth Clatford. The Crook and Shears is the oldest public house in either village. Goodworth Clatford holds one unenviable record – the flying bomb that destroyed the old Royal Oak, the school, the smithy and a row of cottages is said to have been the one that landed the furthest west in England.

Upton Grey

➤ Most of the old houses in Upton Grey are beautiful by any standards, none more so than Beam Ends (17th century), Wayside Cottage and Sycamore Cottage. Almost every house has its good points and the walk up the hill from the tiny village pond to the parish church is a delight.

Note the Norwich Union fire mark on the house named Spinners. Before the days of local authority fire brigades the insurance companies had their own private fire brigades for the protection of their clients' properties. Fire marks or plates on houses were needed for speedy recognition, because the insurance company's brigade would turn out to help only those insured with them. The fire marks were therefore fixed in a conspicuous place on the front of buildings, sufficiently high up to be out of the reach of thieves. The first private fire brigade was that of The Fire Office, which in 1680 had become the earliest fire insurance office. The early fire marks were made of lead and bore the number of the property's insurance policy.

The Old Post House, The Old School House and The Forge, near the pond, were once part of a village scene that must have been busier than it is today. In the 19th century the inhabitants of most villages worked in or around the village, on farms, at big houses, and in shops and trades; today they commute to the nearest towns and some villages are deserted by day.

In 1898, to serve a population of about 300, Upton Grey had three shops, two shoemakers, two blacksmiths, two brick-layers, a baker, a wheelwright, a carrier, a tailor and a publican; that list was typical of any village of that size. Today, with a population of 500, it has one shop and the same public house as in 1898.

The first strange thing to notice about St Mary's church is the exterior wooden stairway to the tower, unique in Hampshire. The second is the very wide brick north aisle of 1715, quite out of proportion to the small nave and even smaller Early English chancel. The brickwork of the aisle is in English bonding (alternate courses of headers and stretchers) and not in Flemish bonding (alternate headers and stretchers in the same course of bricks), which became the more popular style after 1700.

The monument of 1650 to Lady Dorothy Eyre in the chancel is an interesting piece; on a separate tablet is her 30 line 'rhyming' epitaph. In the churchyard two trees are dedicated to Sir Winston Churchill, a maple for his American connections and an oak to represent his own sterling character. From here there is a close view of The Manor House, with its half-timbered bay window, decorative tile-hanging and gabled wings.

The village gets the second part of its name from the family of de Grey, who owned the manor from the 13th to the 15th century. The course of the Roman road from Chichester to Silchester passes through the village, through the grounds of Hoddington House and just to the east of the church.

Vernham Dean

➤ The parish name is Vernhams Dean but the village name is Vernham Dean; formerly it was Ferneham, the 'village or meadow among ferns'. There are four points on the Hampshire boundary where three counties meet, one of them here on the north-east side of the parish at Rockmoor Pond, a secluded little dell just off the road to Ham (a public footpath passes it). It is said that in times of drought the villagers collected their water supply from this pond. Hampshire, Wiltshire and Berkshire meet here, but have done so only since 1895 when the parish of Combe was transferred from Hampshire to Berkshire. (The other three points where three counties meet are at Martin, Hawley and Bramshott.)

The Boot public house at Littledown is a very old inn, built of flint and brick with a thatched roof. It was once a shoemaker's shop-cum-public house, hence its name. It has on display a collection of about 400 boots of every description and material – china, glass, leather, etc – collected and presented from all over the world. Fortunately the collection passes from one innkeeper to the next.

The village has two identical old cast-iron drinking-fountains, one in the churchyard and the other opposite the George Inn, both in working order. The water emerges from a lion's mouth; they are good examples of the sort of Victorian ironwork that is becoming increasingly rare.

Maceys Cottage, not far from St Mary's church, is rather odd. From one side its Gothic-style windows give it a distinctly chapel-like appearance, while from the other side it appears quite normal. When the church was burnt down in 1851 services were held temporarily at the cottage.

A less happy instance of ecclesiastical neighbourliness concerns the Primitive Methodist chapel of 1869, which was built right in front of and within a few feet of the 17th-century Cheyney Cottage, almost completely obscuring its view. This reminds us that there is something to be said for our modern planning regulations.

Warnford

➤ The parish church stands in Warnford Park close to the river Meon, away from the present village. Its dominant feature is the Norman tower, broad and massive with unusual circular bell-openings. Above the south doorway is a Saxon sundial, similar in design to the one at nearby Corhampton.

The church is essentially an aisleless Early English building, with no division between nave and chancel, rebuilt about 1190. On the monument to Sir Thomas Neale and his two wives are their recumbent effigies with the figures of nine of their ten children, kneeling on cushions, four of them carrying skulls to show that they died during their parents' lifetime.

The gravestone in the churchyard to George Lewis depicts a skeleton pointing to a fallen branch of a tree. Legend has it that he was struck down by divine judgement when sawing wood on a Sunday. This story is easily disproved because the date of his death, 17th December 1830, was a Friday.

The remains of King John's House, or St John's House as it should be more correctly called, are behind the church. It was probably built during the reign of King John (1199–1216) it is

Detail of the Neale Monument, Warnford

true, but it belonged to the St John family. It has been a ruin since at least the time of James I.

The 12th Earl of Clanricarde invited the great landscape gardener 'Capability' Brown to have a look at his estate, then known as Belmont. Though there is no documentary evidence it is probable that Brown designed Warnford Park as it exists today.

Warsash

➤ Warsash, like Hamble on the other side of the river, once had a shipbuilding industry. The largest ship ever launched here was HMS *Hotspur*, a 36-gun frigate that took three years to build (1807–10). There is a scale model of it in the south aisle of St Mary's church.

The Rising Sun public house on the waterfront has a strange name for an inn that faces west and from which the rising sun can never be seen. A notice on it states that from a pier opposite the inn on 5th June 1944 3,000 commandos sailed to France in 36 landing-craft. In the leading craft was Brigadier Lord Lovat and his piper, whose music started a wave of cheering that could be heard 'from shore to shore of the Solent'. Opposite the inn is a memorial to the combined operations of British and Allied naval and commando units on D-Day.

Hook is a rare survival of an industrial hamlet, off the beaten track east of Warsash. It consisted originally of a smithy and its house, a wheelwright's shop and house, and a terrace of four cottages (Hook Cottages). The wheelwright's is now a restaurant. Hook Cottages have diamond-shaped window-panes and large chimneys set diagonally. The date 1846 is worked into the cobbled pavement in front of them.

Wellow

➤ The interesting thing about the name Canada, in the south of Wellow parish, is that nobody seems to know its origin. There were no Canadian troops here, nor anybody with Canadian connections. It is said that prize-fights once took place at Boxing Corner, at the junction of Romsey Road and Buttons Lane, because it was near the county boundary; in those days that part of Wellow was in Wiltshire. If the police were seen the boxers fled over the boundary into Hampshire, only a few yards away.

East Wellow church is dedicated to St Margaret of Antioch, a very common dedication of English churches (over 250). In the churchyard is the grave of Florence Nightingale, the obelisk inscribed with the initials F.N. Mementoes of her long life are in the church; she died in London in 1910 at the age of 90, but her family home had been Embley Park in the parish of Wellow. There are several 13th-century wall-paintings in the church, including a St Christopher, a scene from the life of St Margaret and the murder of Thomas Becket.

A few yards west of the crossroads south of Embley Park there is a stone seat with an inscription. The seat was made in 1966 from the stones of a bridge built in 1818, known as the Sounding Arch, which connected two parts of the Embley estate and was often used by Florence Nightingale. There was a legend that a phantom coach and horses could be seen crossing the bridge on New Year's Eve.

West Meon

➤ The village name is two words – West Meon, but the parish name is only one – Westmeon. When first mentioned (in 1284) it was one – Westmenes. It is a much more attractive village than a hurried drive through it would suggest. There are several old timber-framed cottages and two inviting public houses, The Red Lion and The Thomas Lord.

Thomas Lord, the founder of Lord's cricket ground, is commemorated in the public house name because he retired to West Meon in 1830. Two years later he died and was buried in the churchyard. The ashes of Guy Burgess, the defecting diplomat who died in Moscow, are also buried there in the family grave. On the far side of the churchyard are the graves of the parents of Richard Cobden, the famous free trader and co-founder of the Anti-Corn-Law League.

The most famous man ever born at West Meon must be James Thorold Rogers, the eminent 19th-century economist and statistician. His works include *Six Centuries of Work and Wages* and the six-volume *History of Agriculture and Prices in England*. Though a Member of Parliament he was no ranting politician but a diligent fact-finder – we could do with more of his sort today. Earlier he had entered the church, and in 1870 became the first man to withdraw from his vows under the Clerical Disabilities Relief Act. His father, Dr George Rogers, was for more than 40 years a doctor in West Meon. He is commemorated in the village centre by a cross erected by the last surviving of his 16 children.

The church, rebuilt in 1843-6, was George Gilbert Scott's first church in Hampshire. It is an early example of what was then called the 'second pointed' style of the Gothic Revival, ie the transitional period between Early English and Decorated. Scott, though a highly competent architect, was not an individualist; he faithfully reproduced the style of the Middle Ages, as here and later at Highclere. He was in his early thirties when he designed West Meon church, and he went on to build or restore 26 cathedrals and 474 churches, as well as St Pancras Station and the Albert Memorial.

Before the construction of the main road (about 1800) and the railway (1903) West Meon was not an easy place to reach. There was no direct road to Warnford along the valley; travellers went via Lippen Wood and then turned south to Warnford.

The Meon Valley Railway was an ambitious undertaking designed to provide a through route from London to Gosport. Constructed to take double track, it had two tunnels, and a viaduct over the road between East and West Meon. All five passenger stations on this line were of a high standard, canopied red-brick buildings with high-class facilities. (The platforms at West Meon were 565 ft long.) Such a sparsely-inhabited countryside could hardly support a profitable railway, yet passenger trains were not discontinued until 1955.

The site of the old railway station, disused for over 30 years, is a sadly nostalgic spot (see photograph on the cover of this book). The old platforms are now enveloped in vegetation, and weeds sprout from every crack; trees arch across the old trackway to complete a desolate scene. It is said that there was a notice on the platform forbidding the passengers to pick flowers when riding in the train. Though notoriously slow, the trains on this line were not quite as bad as that!

Wherwell

➤ Wherwell is a strange name, first recorded in AD 955 as *Hwerwyl*; according to Ekwall it means 'kettle' or 'cauldron springs', referring perhaps to bubbling springs somewhere. Its pronunciation has always given trouble; locals call it 'Wer-rell' or 'Hurrell'.

The village has a large number of attractive old houses and to identify a few of them implies no criticism of the others. Among the best are Moonflower Cottage and Nos. 18, 19 and 21 Winchester Road, Mole Hall and Nos. 28 and 29 Church Street. The weatherboarded old corn-mill has a first-floor loading doorway.

The parish church was restored in 1856–8, and fragments of the old church can be seen here and there in the village. The Iremonger mausoleum incorporates six grotesque carved heads, and May Cottage in Fullerton Road has a medieval carved head fixed to its end wall.

The Wherwell Home Guard Club on The Old Hill must date from the dark days of the Second World War. The Old Hill was the road to Andover before the present hairpin bend was made in the 19th century to ease the ascent for traffic.

The railway station buildings at Wherwell on the Hurstbourne to Fullerton line (see Longparish) and at Fullerton on the Andover and Redbridge line are both private houses now. There is little trace of the junction at Fullerton where the two lines met. At nearby Testcombe bridge The Mayfly, formerly the Seven Stars Inn, fronting on to the river Test, is one of the most picturesquely sited public houses in the county, and handily situated for walkers on the Test Way.

Whitchurch

➤ Whitchurch was made a free borough by a charter of Winchester Cathedral priory in 1247–9. Its town status lapsed in 1888 but in 1974 it became a town once more. It is situated where since the Middle Ages two important roads have crossed, from Basingstoke to Salisbury and from Newbury to Winchester, and where the latter crosses the river Test.

It has a station on the London to Salisbury railway. It also had one on the defunct Didcot, Newbury and Southampton line; the station building is now a private house.

In the town centre is The White Hart Hotel, an old coaching inn; it was the first overnight stop for travellers from London. Charles Kingsley often stayed there when he came to fish in the Test; he liked the hotel and its food. Opposite is the Georgian town hall, now used by the Midland Bank. Knowing his views on bankers, we can assume that William Cobbett would not have approved of that!

Lord Denning, former Master of the Rolls, was born at No. 5 Newbury Street (his parents' draper's shop) in 1899 and lived there for 24 years. He lives now at The Lawn in Church Street and takes a keen interest in local affairs.

London Street, formerly Mill Street, was once a street of inns, shops and smithies; it has changed quite a bit but many of the old buildings remain. The Red House is a long-established inn, and at the Old School House Lord Denning started his education. Further on, set back between two later houses, is the tiny Voters Cottage, so-named because an Earl of Portsmouth bought it to qualify for a Parliamentary vote. A lane opposite leads to Town Mill on the Test, once a flour mill. At the top of London Street is The Gables, which was built as the Union workhouse in 1847–8.

In Winchester Street is the Silk Mill, built in 1815; its products include gowns for the legal profession. The Kings Arms in Church Street is another old inn, and in Fairclose nearby lived a character nicknamed 'Old Mother Rhubarb' who was for ever watering her plants.

All Hallows church, restored in 1866, has a rare 9th-century Saxon gravestone with a carving of Christ, from the tomb of a lady named Frithburga, who may have been an abbess at a local nunnery.

Wickham

➤ John Leland, the king's antiquary, visited Wickham sometime between 1539 and 1545 and described it as 'a praty townlet where the water brekith into 2 armelettes and goith under 2 wodden bridgges'. Today the water, the river Meon, goes under a brick-and-stone bridge ('Built by subscription 1792') and the other 'armelette' goes under Chesapeake Mill, so named because it was built in 1820 partly with timber from the American warship *Chesapeake*.

Nearby in Bridge Street, on a row of three cottages named The Old Barracks, is an ancient signboard that reads: 'Notice is hereby given That all Vagrants Found in or Near this Place will be Apprehended & Punished with the utmost Severity the Law will Permit. By Order of the Magistrates.' The severity then permitted by the law can only too easily be imagined. The name The Old Barracks is probably derived from their use at some time as officers' quarters. Opposite is Queens Lodge, where Queen Anne is supposed once to have spent a night; it was then a coaching inn.

St Nicholas's church, drastically restored in 1862–3, has a carving of a centaur on one of the capitals of the reset Norman doorway. The Uvedale monument of 1615, though somewhat morbid with its reclining effigies and kneeling children, is resplendent with ornament and emblems.

The Square opens out at right angles to an east-west highway and may have been deliberately planned in that way when a market and fair were granted to Wickham in 1268. The houses round The Square date from medieval to Victorian and are of various heights and sizes; the larger houses are so well placed in relation to the smaller ones that the whole townscape has few equals in Hampshire.

Georgian houses faced with unvitrified silver-grey bricks are a feature of Wickham. On the east side of The Square the two large Georgian houses at the north end, The Old House and its neighbour, are the focal point and really make The Square what it is. On the west side note the timber-framed building with an overhanging upper storey, The King's Head public house (Georgian), and Eastbrook House with its free-standing columns. The early Victorian Ivy Cottage, at the junction of Bridge Street and The Square, is the only visible piece of Gothic architecture and closes the view along the east side admirably.

It is fortunate that Wickham has not sought to emulate its 'twin', Villers-sur-Mer in Normandy. That once-quiet seaside village is now, the guidebooks inform us, an elegant seaside resort, with a casino and everything required for holidays and entertainment. Wickham is fine as it is, and long may it remain so.

Wonston

➤ By the 18th century the rectors of many parish churches were distributing charity on behalf of benefactors. Evidence for this can be found on the many charity and benefaction boards seen on church walls. One here at Holy Trinity church records that in 1710 Dr Thomas Sayer 'gave £30 to the poor which was invested in old South Sea annuities'. Was this the stock that became worthless when the 'South Sea bubble' burst in 1720?

In 1779 John Wickham (his tomb is outside the church) 'gave £5 yearly towards educating poor children'. With this his executors purchased £166 worth of South Sea annuities. A later charity board records that Mrs Cooper Coles left £120 in 1887–92 'to be used by the rector in providing warm clothing for such respectable poor women as he shall in his discretion think fit'.

A church at Wonston was mentioned in a grant to New Minster, Winchester, in AD 901; this makes it the earliest recorded church in Hampshire. It has suffered two disastrous fires, in 1714 and again in 1908 when it was largely destroyed. Faulty heating might cause a fire in winter but surely not in summer. In 1908 the fire occurred one night in August; the church had until then been left open day and night, which suggests other possible causes of the fire.

Wootton St Lawrence

◄ A memorial window in St Lawrence's church commemorates Charles Butler, rector from 1600 to 1647, who wrote a famous book on bees entitled *The Feminine Monarchie, or a Treatise concerning Bees* (1609). The first English book on bees was published in 1574; Butler's book was the first to show that a hive was ruled by a queen and not by a king, as had previously been supposed. The third edition of his book (1634) was written in phonetic spelling, of which he was a strong advocate.

A man of some learning, Butler also wrote books on rhetoric, English grammar, spelling reform, music, and affinity as a bar to marriage. The final words from his book on music are engraved on a panel of the window.

> Live Soberly Righteously and Holily
> Holily in respect to God
> Righteously in respect of our neighbours
> Soberly in respect of ourselves.

The splendid monument to Sir Thomas Hooke, showing him reclining in armour, is by the famous sculptor Roubiliac. When the church was restored in 1864 small carved stone heads were placed on various parts of the interior and exterior. There are 18 of them – see how many you can find.

The barn by the roadside a few yards from the church has a delicate weather-vane in the shape of a horse and plough.

Yateley

→ Yateley is one of Hampshire's newest towns; its population has increased from 1,238 in 1891 to about 20,000 now. It began to expand outwards from the old village centre near the church in the 19th century, but many of the large houses built then have had to make way for post-war housing estates, which form the greater part of modern Yateley.

St Peter's church suffered a disastrous fire in 1979 but remarkably the wooden tower escaped serious damage. This was fortunate because it is one of the best timber-framed towers in Hampshire – the inside reveals a veritable forest of beams and supports. The lich-gate is a rare example of the type that pivots in the centre; in Sussex this type is known as a tapsell gate.

Yateley Common is one of the largest commons in the county. Wyndham's Pool, reached from Cricket Hill Lane, is a delightful little pond, an 18th-century fishpond reservoir; a nature trail starts here. The damp conditions near the pond encourage the growth of mosses, ferns and trees, in contrast to the dry, infertile heathland that covers much of the common. The area around the nearby houses is known as Brandy Bottom – probably a relic of the days when smuggling was rife on the main road. From the A30 you can turn off to Stroud's Pond, another secluded spot, where you may see vividly-coloured toadstools.

Selected Bibliography

This is a list of some of the most useful of the many reference books that have been consulted in the preparation of this book.

Allen R. and Dine D. *Ringwood Seen and Remembered* Hampshire County Library 1985

Barton J. *The Visitor's Guide to Hampshire and the Isle of Wight* Moorland Publishing 1985

Beddington W. and Christy E. *It Happened in Hampshire* The Hampshire Federation of Women's Institutes 1977

Beresford D. *Nether Wallop in Hampshire* R. N. K. Beresford 1973

Bosworth J. *Bishop's Waltham in old picture postcards* European Library 1985

Brode A. *The Hampshire Village Book* Countryside Books 1985

Butterfield R. P. *Monastery and Manor: The History of Crondall* E. W. Langham, Farnham 1948

Cobbett W. *Rural Rides* new edition Reeves and Turner 1908

Cochrane C. *The lost Roads of Wessex* David and Charles 1969

Coles R. *The Story of Lymington* Local Heritage Books 1983

Course E. *The Railways of Southern England: The Main Lines* 1973: *Secondary and Branch Lines* 1974: *Independent and Light Railways* 1976 Batsford

Cox J. G. *Castleman's Corkscrew* City of Southampton 1975

Crawford O. G. S. *Archaeology in the Field* Phoenix House 1954

Crawford O. G. S. *A Short History of Nursling* Warren and Son 1948

Curtis W. *A Short History and Description of the Town of Alton* Warren and Son/Simpkin & Co 1896

Defoe D. *A Tour Thro' the whole Island of Great Britain* 1724–6 reprinted Peter Davies 1927

Dictionary of National Biography Oxford University Press 1949–86

Drew J. S. *Compton Near Winchester* Warren and Son 1939

Dunlop G. D. *Pages from the History of Highclere* The Holywell Press 1940

Dyer J. *Southern England: an Archaeological Guide* Faber and Faber 1973

Ekwall E. *The Concise Oxford Dictionary of English Place-Names* Oxford University Press 4th edition 1960

Ellis M. (ed) *Water and Wind Mills in Hampshire and the Isle of Wight* Southampton Univ. Industrial Archaeo. Group 1978

Farrugia J. *The Letter Box* Centaur Press 1969

Gilpin W. *Remarks on Forest Scenery* R. Blamire 1791

Goldsmith J. *Hambledon* Winton Publications 1971

Gorsky D. *The old village of Hartley Wintney* Hartley Wintney Preservation Society 1973

Green A. R. and Green P. M. *Saxon Architecture and Sculpture in Hampshire* Warren and Son 1951

Hadfield C. *The Canals of South and South East England* David and Charles 1969

Hagen M. *Annals of Old Ropley* C. Mills, Alton 1929

Hampshire Chronicle 1772–1989

Hampshire, the County Magazine Paul Cave Pubns. 1960–89

Hampshire Field Club Papers and Proceedings 1885–1988

Hampshire Treasures Survey Hampshire County Council 1979–86

Harley J.B. and O'Donoghue Y. *The Old Series Ordnance Survey Maps of England and Wales: 1 inch to 1 mile* H. Margary 1981

Hatcher Review, The Vol. 3 No. 27 Hatcher Review Trust 1989

Hawkes B. *A Walk round old Whitchurch* Figuredene 1981

Hawkins C. W. *The Story of Alton* Alton U.D.C. 1973

Hardcastle F. *Records of Burley* Chameleon International 1987

Henderson I. *Philippi's Crawley* Ian T. Henderson 1977

Hill R. *A History of Stockbridge* J.A.C. Publications 1976

Hughes M. (ed) *The Small Towns of Hampshire* Hampshire Archaeological Committee 1976

Jones J. S. T. *Headley* The Gresham Press

Kelly's Directory of Hampshire and the Isle of Wight various editions Kelly's Directories

Kemp B. *English Church Monuments* Batsford 1980

King E. *A Walk through Lymington* Kings of Lymington 1972

Lane-Poole E.H. *Damerham and Martin* Compton Russell 1976

Larwood J. and Hotten J. C. *English Inn Signs* Chatto and Windus 1951

Leland J. *The Itinerary* (ed. L. T. Smith) Centaur Press 1964

Matthews W. H. *Mazes and Labyrinths* Longmans, Green & Co 1922

Moore P. (ed) *A Guide to the Industrial Archaeology of Hampshire and the Isle of Wight* Southampton University Industrial Archaeology Group 1984

Moore P. *The Industrial Heritage of Hampshire and the Isle of Wight* Phillimore & Co 1988

Morris J. (ed) *Domesday Book: Hampshire* Phillimore & Co 1982

Mott R. A. *Henry Cort: The Great Finer* The Metals Soc. 1983

Newman R. C. *A Hampshire Parish: Bramshott and Liphook* Frank Westwood 1976

O'Connell G. *Secretive Southwick* Willowbridge 1984

Ogilby J. *Britannia* John Ogilby 1675

Perkins W. F. *Boldre* King's Library, Lymington 1935

Pevsner N. and Lloyd D. *The Buildings of England: Hampshire and the Isle of Wight* Penguin Books 1967

Reger A. J. *A Short History of Emsworth and Warblington* 1967

Robinson N. *Hamble* Kingfisher Railway Productions 1987

Rolt L. T. C. *Waterloo Ironworks* David and Charles 1969

Routh M. *Amport* 1986

Shurlock B. *Portrait of the Solent* Robert Hale 1983

Shurlock B. *The Solent Way* Hampshire County Council 1984

Shurlock B. *The Test Way & The Clarendon Way* Hampshire County Council 1986

Smith J. H. *Grayshott* Frank Westwood 1978

Standfield F. G. *A History of East Meon* Phillimore & Co 1984

Stone R. A. *The Meon Valley Railway* Kingfisher Railway Productions 1983

Tavener L. E. *The Common Lands of Hampshire* Hampshire County Council 1957

Thomas F. S. G. *The King holds Hayling* Pelham, Havant 1961

Thruxton Village Assn. *A Parish Appraisal: Thruxton* Thruxton Association & Appraisal Committee 1981

Titchfield History Society *Titchfield: A History* Titchfield History Society 1982

The Victoria History of the Counties of England: Hampshire and the Isle of Wight Archibald Constable & Co 1900–14

Vine P. A. L. *London's Lost Route to Basingstoke* David and Charles 1968

Welch E. *The Bankrupt Canal: Southampton and Salisbury* City of Southampton 1966

White G. *The Natural History and Antiquities of Selborne* B. White & Son 1789

White W. *History, Gazetteer and Directory of Hampshire and the Isle of Wight* various editions William White

Whiteman W. M. *The Edward Thomas Country* Paul Cave Pubns.

Williams B. *Fire Marks and Insurance Office Fire Brigades* Charles and Edwin Layton 1927

Wise J. *The New Forest: its History and its Scenery* Smith, Elder & Co 1863

Index

In more than a hundred of the places in this book some mention is made of the parish church, most often to describe graves, tombs, memorials and monuments, and therefore these are not listed in the index.

Pilgrims' Way 16, 145
Pillar-boxes 54, 117, 151
Pilot Hill 60
Pitt, Thomas 9
Plestor, The 147
Plymouth Brethren 48, 148
Poorhouses 34, 58, 77, 82, 137, 147
Portal, Henry 98
Portchester 138
Portuguese Fireplace 119
Post office 39, 97
Priories 29, 76, 121, 154
Priors Dean 139
Pulpits 14, 18, 21, 56, 58, 116, 118, 148
Pym, John 28

Quakers 10
Quarley 139
Quays 61, 63, 68, 106

Railways 18, 27, 30, 33, 45, 84, 92, 100, 102, 104, 128, 130, 134, 176, 178, 179
Railway stations 18, 33, 83, 84, 88, 104, 114, 126, 128, 130, 138, 151, 176, 178
Rectors 22, 42, 44, 45, 47, 64, 67, 90, 92, 113, 126, 142, 146, 149, 156, 182
Ringwood 141
Riots, agricultural workers 11, 82, 147
River, Itchen 92, 133, 169
  Meon 58, 66, 113, 166, 180
  Test 98, 105, 135, 158, 168, 179
Roads, medieval and coach 16, 38, 79, 110, 122, 135, 139, 145, 155, 179
Roads, Roman 80, 110, 160, 171
Roads, turnpike 18, 34, 38, 106, 169

Roberts, Henry 125
Rockbourne 142
Rockmoor Pond 173
Rodney, Admiral 133
Rogers, James Thorold 177
Romsey 143
Rookery Dell 121
Ropley 145
Rowlands Castle 145

St Boniface 130
St Mary Bourne 146
St Mary Magdalen Hospital 42
Salt industry 106
School, 'dame' 75
Schools, village 11, 22, 31, 45, 50, 58, 61, 62, 67, 70, 74, 80, 82, 84
Schultze, Eduard 70
Scott, George Gilbert 83, 176
Selborne 147
'Shakers' 87
Shawford 45
Shaw, George Bernard 72
Sherborne St John 148
Shipyards 37, 101, 175
Silchester 149
Signs, village 16, 64
Small, John 137
Smuggling 40, 63, 106, 183
Soberton 151
Solent Way 106
Sopley 152
Southey, Robert 22, 106
South Hayling 152
Southwick 154
Spenser, Edmund 10
Stage-coaches 10, 152
Stained glass 26, 58, 71, 123, 126, 148
Stead, W. T. 153
Steele, Anne 32
Steep 155
Steventon 156